SIR
PETER
SCOTT
at 80

A Retrospective

All royalties to

**THE
WILDFOWL
& WETLANDS TRUST**

SIR PETER SCOTT at 80

A Retrospective

ALAN SUTTON
in association with
CHELTENHAM ART GALLERY AND MUSEUMS
1989

ALAN SUTTON PUBLISHING
30 BRUNSWICK ROAD · GLOUCESTER

ALAN SUTTON PUBLISHING INC
WOLFEBORO · NEW HAMPSHIRE · USA

British Library Cataloguing in Publication Data

Sir Peter Scott at 80.
    1. Ornithology. Scott, Sir, Peter, 1909–
    598'.092'4

    ISBN 0-86299-651-1

Library of Congress Cataloging in Publication Data applied for

Cover pictures: front: The Boundary Dyke in Spring; *back: Peter
with Hawaiian Geese (Ne-Nes) at Slimbridge*

Typesetting and origination by
Alan Sutton Publishing Limited
Colour origination by Spa Graphics
Printed in Great Britain by
Dotesios Printers Ltd

ACKNOWLEDGEMENTS

This book has been published to accompany the retrospective exhibition of Sir Peter Scott's work organised by Cheltenham Art Gallery and Museums, a department of Cheltenham Borough Council.

The exhibition and book would not have been possible without the generous cooperation and help of Sir Peter and Lady Scott, and especially Sir Peter's editing of the catalogue notes and permission to quote from his books. Particular thanks are due to Jonathan Benington, who wrote the biography and catalogue to each chapter, and George Breeze, Gallery Director. Special thanks are also due to the owners of paintings and to the contributors. Many have provided help and advice including June White, without whom this book would never have got off the ground, Stephen Myall and Ackermann & Son Ltd, Lord Buxton, Joe Blossom, Michael Ounsted, Cassandra Phillips, Commander David Joel, Paul Walkden, Sally Nunn, William Marler, The Honourable D.E.H. Bigham, Michael Benington, Eliot and Nicola Starks, Lynn Knight and the staff of Cheltenham Reference and Lending Libraries, and others who prefer to remain unnamed.

'Animals of all sorts have always followed him as if he were another Orpheus.'

Lord Kennet of the Dene, from the introduction to *Portrait Drawings* (*Country Life*, 1949)

CONTENTS

CATALOGUE NOTE

All pictures are by Peter Scott unless otherwise stated.

Measurements are given in inches followed, in brackets, by centimetres, height preceding width.

HRH Princess Elizabeth and the Hon. Director (Peter Scott) by the Narrowboat *Beatrice*, a floating hostel on the Gloucester–Sharpness Canal, in March 1950

The names of those lenders who wished to be acknowledged are given, otherwise the ownership is marked as private.

PREFACE

I cannot remember a time when I did not draw. My mother, who was a pupil of Rodin, and became a professional sculptor of distinction, strongly encouraged me to do so. At the age of three I used to lie face down on my nursery floor drawing animals and aeroplanes and ships. Ever since then I have felt deprived if I have not been able to draw or paint something every day. Practice does not necessarily make perfect, wherein perhaps lies the fascination. I am perpetually aware of my limitations as a draughtsman and painter. But my delight in the beauty of living creatures, especially birds, sometimes creeps into my work and leaves an image which others seem to enjoy.

To have a retrospective exhibition, which I have not had before, is very flattering and agreeable to an octogenarian naturalist, and to have a book in which many of the works are reproduced makes it even better because books last longer than exhibitions. It is also very nice to find a biographical section, a bibliography, and contributions from nine of my life-long friends.

From these you may gather that my life has been hugely enjoyable, fortunate and happy. For the last forty years of it, I have to praise and thank my adored wife Philippa, my three children and seven grand-children.

SIR PETER SCOTT CH CBE DSC FRS
Slimbridge, June 1989

The things I am and have been most proud of

1. My paintings – Being able to sell the majority of my pictures at an Exhibition both in 1933 and 1989, and at many exhibitions in between.

2. My books. Having written eighteen and illustrated twenty others.

3. The creation of the Wildfowl Trust and its development, with seven Centres in the UK.

4. My part in the creation of the World Wildlife Fund (World Wide Fund for Nature).

5. The *Look* programmes on television (seventeen years) and *Nature Parliament* on radio (twenty-one years).

6. Winning the Prince of Wales Cup for International 14ft dinghies three times (1937, 1938 and 1946), the last two with John Winter as joint helmsman.

7. Winning a Bronze Medal in Olympic yachting (single-handed sailing) – 1936.

8. Winning the British Gliding Championship in 1963.

9. Coming second in the America's Cup in 1964.

10. Becoming First Lieutenant of a Destroyer in World War II – 1941.

11. Becoming Senior Officer of a Flotilla of SGBs in World War II – 1943.

12. Being appointed to command a new frigate in World War II – 1945.

13. Being awarded two DSCs and being mentioned three times in Despatches in World War II.

14. Being awarded an MBE for inventing a night camouflage scheme for ships – 1942.

15. Being awarded a CBE in 1953 for work connected with the Wildfowl Trust.

16. Building up the Species Survival Commission of IUCN and inventing the Red Data Books, listing endangered species.

17. Being awarded the first Knighthood for Conservation in 1973.

18. Being elected Rector of Aberdeen University by the student body – 1960.

19. Being appointed Chancellor of the University of Birmingham by the Senate and serving in that capacity for ten years (from 1974).

20. Being appointed a Companion of Honour by HM The Queen (limited to sixty-five people) and a Fellow of the Royal Society, both honours being awarded in June 1987.

PETER SCOTT

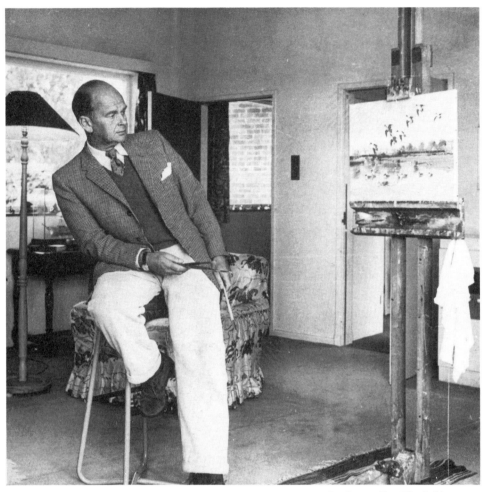

In the studio, Slimbridge

FOREWORD

by KEITH SHACKLETON

The first original 'Scotts' I ever saw turned up while rummaging in a cupboard at school. I was thirteen or thereabouts.

Generations of boys had kept their artistic bits and pieces in this cupboard, which formed the main storage place in a deconsecrated tin chapel, reincarnated as an overflow studio and now (alas) long since demolished.

The originals were drypoint etchings on copper plates and must have lain there unnoticed for the fourteen years that separated Peter Scott's and my own attendance at Oundle, with its regular sessions of creative encouragement known as 'voluntary studio'.

The Studio differed from the Art Room proper in many ways. The Art Room was somewhat sanitised and institutional – a parquet floor, tidily stacked drawing boards, lay-figures on window ledges. Geometric forms for studies in perspective were arranged on polished tables and a plaster *Venus de Milo* for interpretation of the freer line. There was a stuffed Osprey I remember, and a bust of Voltaire whose sickly likeness we tried to capture in vain. Everything was geared to formal instruction and whole classes attended at a time.

Drawing was a gift, we were told – but a

measure of success lay within the grasp of all. Encouragement was a key-word. We saw art teachers more as entertainers than pedagogues, and despite conformity to a rigid discipline they made the weekly art class a welcome break from Latin tags or trigonometry. We assessed Art as level-pegging with the evil smells and minor explosions that delighted us so much in the chemistry labs. But it was none the less 'school'.

The much-loved 'Tin Tabernacle' – the Studio – was something else. Mysterious and exciting things happened. All the sets for the school plays were designed, built and painted there. It was down by a wood and a long walk from the centre of things. There was a badger sett and one could hear the animals snuffling about under the floor boards.

Here, freedom of expression was propagated by an expert from willing pupils, allowed to do their own thing. The 'Studio boys' had seen the light – or certainly we thought we had. We were volunteers; Art Rooms were for conscripts. Moreover nothing could have lain hidden for a *week* in the Art Room cupboards, let alone fourteen years. So, not surprisingly, it was in the Studio that Peter Scott had taken off. . . .

An eager group surrounded the printing press as we were shown how plates were inked and impressions taken on special absorbent paper. The first subject to emerge was a lizard; another a hawk-moth. There was a kingfisher on a willow stem and a fat trout rising eagerly to a fly – but alas, no geese.

91. Portrait of Sir Peter Scott, by Dafila Scott, 1989 (p. 127)

40.   Pinkfeet, 1945 (p. 51)

Painting in what is now the
Curator's house, Slimbridge,
c. 1949

By then *Morning Flight* had been published, if
not *Wild Chorus* as well, so we were unprepared for
such an omission. Peter Scott paints *geese*. We all
knew it as a simple truth and several of us had been
inspired and tried to do the same. We also knew
that Corot painted willow trees, Munnings horses,
Montague Dawson windjammers and Farqua-
harson sheep at sunset (but always in snow because
he had problems drawing their feet). Had the
plates not been clearly signed 'P.S.' we would have
doubted their authenticity.

But not withstanding the absence of geese, the
drypoints carried a very special significance. 'Make

the boy interested in Natural History,' had written the infant Peter's father, Robert Falcon Scott, in his last Antarctic letter to his wife, 'It's better than games. They teach it at some schools.' Had he lived another twelve years, the moth, the lizard, the kingfisher and the rising trout would have spelled for him a happy fulfilment – sure testimony to a deep and burgeoning interest, broadly based.

For those entranced by living creatures and blessed with an ability to draw, subjects decide themselves, demonstrating at the same time the strength of the motivation behind eàch one. Small wonder too, that increasing knowledge and feeling for a subject, combined with increasing skill as an artist will lead to more convincing interpretations of the truth. The wider and more immediate the interest, the more varied the subjects – I am reminded of Motor Torpedo Boats racing through the night, lit by star shells and laced with red and green streams of tracer, in Peter's book *The Battle of the Narrow Seas*. But it was always animals, in one form or another, that took pride of place.

A Life Fellowship of the Zoological Society of London, given as a christening present by his godfather, J.M. Barrie, was a flying start for Peter. His first published work was an illustration – a Privet Hawk Moth caterpillar – for a book of insects. References for such drawings were easily come by. He was never without the companionship of moths in boxes, mice in cages, fish in tanks and a lizard in the pocket.

Formal art training followed Oundle and Cam-

Keith Shackleton and Peter extricating the 30 White-fronts and 1 Pinkfoot after the first rocket net catch ever made – on the New Grounds at Slimbridge, 1948

bridge; first at the State Academy in Munich and later at the Royal Academy Schools in London. It would be interesting to know at what stage the enviable ability to write and draw equally well with either hand crept into his growing catalogue of attainments. Peter, in common with a surprisingly large proportion of gifted artists, is left handed. But an extremely competent right is there in reserve.

In the years after the war, he and I painted quite often on the same picture. Occasionally it was a case of stark necessity, with a deadline set on the picture and time running out. His left hand and my right proved quite a bonus in that he could work on the right side of the canvas and I on the left, our brush handles occasionally clacking together in the middleground like the bills of courting gannets.

But the overall plan was always his, as was the final brushwork. This part became known as 'Scotting over', on the laudable ground of artistic integrity – that a Scott is a Scott, and no nonsense. But it led to years of happy subterfuge and poker-faced denials. I occasionally thought a picture of mine looked a bit better one morning and attributed it to a more tolerant appraisal – little knowing! By way of retribution I learned to make minor adjustments on his easel too, of which several, I am happy to say, passed unnoticed. . . .

Peter would be the first to admit that there is little future in acquiring skills unless they are used. To him an Art School training implied no more than a heightened capability to portray what he truly cared about – natural spectacle, moments that afforded a special joy. Nor would he flinch from admitting that much of this spectacle – mist and half-light, birds moving over reflecting mud, extravagant dawns and golden sunsets – was first witnessed over the coaming of a gun-punt. There is a deep-down, primeval urge throughout all mankind, for the hunter – if he has the skill – to portray his quarry. I believe it can most easily be explained as a gesture of gratitude to the animal itself and homage to the god that put it there.

Whatever its origins in his case, *Morning Flight* was the first revelation of his painting imperative. Moreover, the book was a milestone in the unfolding history of bird painting.

If one had to dredge up an influence on Peter's painting, rather than attributing it to something totally original, the nearest would be the great Swedish painter Bruno Liljefors. There is a certain similarity of approach – animals in their landscape as a cohesive entity, enriched by the union of both elements. Somehow it made the established animal portrait look dated, a record rather than a picture. There was another factor. Without realising it, the Wright brothers had made a significant contribution to the painting and understanding of birds, simply by introducing an awareness of aerodynamics. Lift and trim, drag and stall are vital factors in birds, giving them a dimension above all other warm-blooded creatures but bats. Before aeroplanes showed the way, the great painters seemed to accept merely that birds had wings. They painted them with meticulous clarity when at rest, but seemed reluctant to be drawn on the specifics of what happened when the wings were actually flapped and the birds passed through the air.

Peter's loyalty to his chosen subject is legendary and the reason is simple enough: with care and thought and renewed observation there is *always* something more that can be distilled from a subject, no matter how familiar it has become over the years. So the 'Peter-Scott-paints-geese' dictum is nothing if not understandable. It began in the twenties and still goes strong, even though it is now well over forty years since the last hint of hunting fervour was laid aside. In its place there may have been an ingredient of making amends:

Keith Shackleton in
Shackleton's hut at Cape
Royds, Antarctica, 1971

converts tend to show heightened commitment.
But more realistically, it seems that a long and
self-punishing dedication to conservation is just
another by-product of caring very deeply about
wild animals in their own right, especially in the
context of their present predicament, rather than
just as lovely subjects for pictures.

So wildfowl keep happening on the canvas.
They are and always have been the main stream.
Painting them is like touching base. Here is a
subject completely understood, drawing on a
memory bank of four score years, recalled, selec-

ted and pieced together in planned composition. There will be limitless changes in light, in grouping, direction, background. And because the exercise is so familiar there go with it all the pleasures and laid-back assurance of working close to home. A picture painted for sheer enjoyment is still a picture of wildfowl.

Conformity to the mainstream however, is something that would never appeal on any permanent basis. There has to be experiment. Adventure and escape are built-in potentials of any new, white canvas.

To feel closer to the lifestyle of birds, Peter felt obliged to fly aeroplanes and soar in gliders – with, incidentally, an indecent display of skill. To indulge a fascination for whales and reef fishes he had to become a diver and share their element on a proper basis. Artistically, each new realm of understanding showed in his pictures because each one sprang from the authentic; they displayed the conviction of a personal experience translated into paint.

For years now, Peter has kept diaries of his travels. They are fat little books about the size of a Field Guide, made fatter by the inclusion of Philippa's photographs, clippings from newspapers, notes and letters, and retained from bursting by a stout elastic band. Extracts have been published in the last few years; but the clinical selection of tit-bits – which is, I suppose, inevitable – gives no hint of the original character of the books nor yet of the author himself. With handwriting as clear and legible as any typewriter, a chance was missed to reproduce in facsimile, with all the random annotations that display the kind of detail that passes through an alert mind in a wild place, when there is a pencil in hand to record it.

All representational painters who have a special subject allegiance, have their favourites within general parameters and Peter is no exception. Because of the varied richness of the animal kingdom however, his particular preferences tend to be wider spaced than most. Returning to the thought of drawing as a personal statement of gratitude, it comes as no surprise to find him painting montage-type compositions that embody all his favourites in one. In these, size and respective scale is of no importance; design is what counts. The intricate wing pattern of an insect can be given greater prominence than a herd of migrating wildebeest. The abstract values lurking in realism have always exerted a fascination, while the realism itself betrays tender evidence of love, respect and admiration.

Running through his work there is always hope. Art's more doom-laden messages are noteworthy only for their absence.

He is deferential towards abstract painting and has toyed with it himself – but expects to see some evidence of skill in it before taking it too seriously. He would have found himself in complete accord with Picasso – a self-confessed puller of legs and a brilliant painter who 'exhausted as best he could the imbecility, the vanity, the cupidity of his contemporaries'. Peter Scott will play with colour and play with shape, for the fun of it. The *serious* business is all about truth – painted with sincerity.

'I'll never be a great painter,' he once said in his early twenties, 'not even a very good one.' And because of the vagaries of self-denigration, these are issues best left to others to decide. 'Good' has no real meaning because it is dependent upon comparisons and the volatility of personal taste. 'Sincerity' on the other hand, is easier to define: it means to paint from the heart.

1 EARLY YEARS

Peter Markham Scott was born on 14 September 1909 in the family house at 174 Buckingham Palace Road. His father, Robert Falcon Scott, died two and a half years later on the way back from the South Pole, having reached it on 17 January 1912, thirty-four days after Amundsen's Norwegian party. The news of his death only broke a year later when Kathleen Scott was on board ship and hoping to meet her husband in New Zealand.

Peter's mother was an accomplished sculptor who had studied under Rodin in Paris and was familiar with painters such as Henry Tonks and Charles Shannon. She encouraged her son's drawing and took to heart the words her husband wrote in the Antarctic a few days before he died: 'Make the boy interested in Natural History. It is better than games. They encourage it at some schools. . . .' However, she was careful not to impose the subject too forcefully on her son, preferring subtly to bring him into contact with biologists and naturalists such as Sir Ray Lankester, who fostered the boy's curiosity by giving him problem specimens to identify, describe and draw.

Peter aged about four

Before the First World War Peter enjoyed discovering plants and animals for himself during holidays at Sandwich in Kent. Here he was attracted by marine life, lizards and moths and he saw his first wild geese, a skein of Brents. While at West Downs, a prep school near Winchester, he learned how to find and identify Hawk Moth caterpillars and began to take a serious interest in birds. Being able to experience animals at first hand was the key to his fascination, whether this meant fishing for Rudd-Bream hybrids in a local pond or keeping tame owls and bats.

In 1922 Kathleen Scott married Edward Hilton Young, a war hero and Member of Parliament who later became a Cabinet Minister and accepted a peerage as Lord Kennet of the Dene. He had an idyllic thatched cottage called The Lacket in the village of Lockeridge in Wiltshire, at which Peter often stayed, walking in the woods and denes and collecting wild flowers. They both shared an interest in the natural sciences in general and birds in particular, and although he had lost an arm in the War Peter's step-father was very adept at sailing small boats and gave the boy his first lessons. At this time the family had started to holiday regularly on the Norfolk Broads, an ideal environment in which Peter could develop his enthusiasms for sailing and water birds.

At the age of fourteen he went to Oundle School near Peterborough, which was renowned for its enlightened attitude towards science and technology. Apart from the study of biology and animal life his other interests at this time were skating, drawing and choral singing. Drawing had been an enjoyable pastime from a very early age. At first zoo animals, hot-air balloons, ships and aeroplanes captured his imagination, but at Oundle

Peter with Zonure (Spiny Lizard), *c.* 1920

the emphasis was very much on insects, birds and reptiles. A natural talent enabled him to make tidy and accurate drawings in the dissection room, while he lost no opportunity to draw live specimens too. The art master at Oundle was the Irish painter E.M.O'R. Dickie who, when shown a drawing of a kestrel by Peter, advised him to draw a pudding. The lesson was memorable because of the difficulties posed by the rounded, symmetrical subject. In 1924 Peter had his first drawings published in a book by Evelyn Cheesman, *Everyday Doings of Insects*, which was followed by a volume he illustrated entirely with his own drawings. *Adventures Among Birds* was a collaboration by three schoolboys – Michael Dilke who wrote the text, Peter who drew the marginal illustrations, and John Brereton who arranged for the book's publication.

After leaving school in 1927, Peter furthered his ambition to be a biologist by going to Trinity College, Cambridge to study zoology, botany, physiology and geology. His spare time was divided between sailing, skating, beagling, painting and wildfowling, and increasingly the outdoor experience of wild places and animals appealed to him more than academic study. From Cambridge he wrote to his stepfather:

It's such a rare thing to be able to enjoy and understand a wild place. . . . Anyone can learn the names of fossils and the classifications of animals but I don't want to do things that anyone can do. Anyone can't paint – and I

3

suppose that's why I like it. . . . I suppose it's scope for the imagination that I want and there isn't any that I can find in the inside of a dogfish.

The realisation that the artistic and adventurous aspects of his personality might be suppressed led to Peter's decision to become an artist, and accordingly he switched to the History of Art and Architecture in his second year at university. He held his first exhibition of paintings in a Cambridge shop and published pictures of wildfowl for the first time in 1929, in *Country Life* magazine. On 17 December 1930 he took his degree and on the same afternoon went snipe shooting with a friend.

Now that art and wildfowl were Peter's two most absorbing interests, he decided to train to be a professional painter. He was already a skilled draughtsman but wanted the stimulus of being alongside other budding artists and studying anatomy, perspective, the human model and the Old Masters. To this end, in 1931, he enrolled in the Munich Academy, studying for a term in the animal painting class of Angelo Jank. However, the animals involved were horses, pigs and goats, and when Peter showed the Professor his very first oil painting, featuring geese against a sunrise, Herr Jank could not understand why he had painted it. It was, perhaps, a less than promising beginning.

While in Munich Peter learned German and became a passionate devotee of the opera and Wagner. He also flew to Berlin to attend the World Skating Championships to watch one of his girlfriends, who was the American Champion Maribel Vinson. Also watching as a sports reporter was the then journalist Paul Gallico. Peter later told him about his lighthouse home and a wild Pink-footed Goose which came there two years running. Paul subsequently used the story as a basis for his bestseller, *The Snow Goose*, which much later Peter illustrated. While there Bernard Adams, the great British skating coach, who knew Peter was already a very good free skater, offered to make him world champion if he would do nothing else for two years. But Peter declined the offer, returning to London in the summer and becoming a pupil at the Royal Academy School on 15 December 1931. His studentship lasted until June 1933 and his teachers were Walter Monnington, Francis Jackson and Walter Russell.

During his Cambridge days and into the 1930s the Fens of Cambridgeshire and salt marshes of Norfolk were the setting for most of the wildfowling adventures of Peter and his companions – Michael Dilke, Christopher Dalgety, Michael Bratby, David Haig Thomas and John Winter. They had met either at school or university and all shared an addiction for being out on the marshes at dawn and dusk, waiting perhaps for the dawn flight of geese over the sea wall to their feeding grounds, or drifting down on the tide over the mudflats in a duck-punt and having to wait for the flood tide till they could return. The geese which came to that part of the country in winter were mainly Pink-footed and White-fronted Geese. Peter wrote of their magic:

They are mysterious birds coming from far-away northern lands, impelled by an unknown force and kept infallibly on their course by an unknown sense. They are wild and wary birds, a traditional quarry of man from immemorial times. Their flight is swift and their formations fill the sky, but I believe that their greatest appeal is to the ear. . . . The nightingale and the blackcap and the curlew are nature's soloists but the geese are her chorus, as rousing, over the high sand, as the 'Sanctus' of Bach's B Minor Mass.

To get close to the ducks and geese and experience the wild places they inhabited at the most beautiful times of day counted for much more than any satisfaction derived from shooting them. Sometimes the expeditions resulted in a large 'bag' but equally often no birds were killed.

In later life Peter gave up shooting after an incident when a wounded goose was stranded on soft mud and could not be rescued. But already in the early 1930s he was becoming concerned about conservation issues and began to be more interested in catching geese and ducks alive than in hunting them. In the spring of 1932 he started saving geese which were shot but not killed. He also devised a special net thrown over by powerful springs, and later by rockets, which could be set in a field where geese were likely to feed, though it required much patience and experimenting before the first bird was caught. Netting geese proved at least as exciting and difficult as attempting to shoot them, and with the added bonus of being able to

Burying the rocket for goose catching and ringing, *c.* 1950

44. Emperor Geese, 1947 (p. 69)

45.   Snow Geese flying by moonlight, 1947 (p. 69)

tame the birds and make friends with them (the technique of ringing and marking birds was then still in its infancy but later became the main objective of the rocket nets).

It was in March 1932 that Peter first discovered the art of decoying, when he visited Borough Fen Decoy at Peakirk, which had been operated by the Williams family since the seventeenth century. The duck decoy consisted of a pond from which radiated eight curved tapering ditches or 'pipes'. Each ditch was covered with a net and flanked by a series of overlapping screens which could be seen through from one direction but not the other. By putting out food for the ducks on the landings of the ditch the birds could be lured into the pipe, and then flushed by the sudden appearance of the decoyman at the mouth of the pipe. Alternatively, a dog or cat would be made to appear between the screens, enticing the birds towards it on the principle that a group of small animals is often not afraid to approach a would-be predator. The ducks were caught once they had flown to the end of the net. Some thousands of ducks were caught in this device and sent to market in those days. Now the decoy is operated by the Wildfowl and Wetlands Trust which Peter created, and the birds are caught for ringing and immediate release.

Peter went to live at Borough Fen Decoy at the end of 1932 and designed an observation hut for it so that he could watch the ducks at close quarters. That winter he painted about forty pictures of wildfowl there and showed them the following summer in his first London exhibition.

Catalogue

1. HMS *Victory*

1923

Etching 5 × 4 (12.6 × 10.1)
Private collection

2. Eyed Lizard (*Lacerta ocellata*)

March 1924

Pen and watercolour 7⅛ × 4⁹⁄₁₆ (18.1 × 11.6)
Private collection

This picture of an eyed lizard, *Lacerta ocellata*, was drawn on notepaper of The Lacket, the cottage in Wiltshire which belonged to Peter's stepfather, Edward Hilton Young. The lizard was one Peter caught during a holiday on the island of Noirmoutier off the mouth of the Loire and brought back to school. He called it 'Moctaques'.

3. Brent Geese at the Bedford Levels

1929

Watercolour 14 × 20 (35.6 × 50.8)
Mrs John Faber

The artist's earliest pictures of wildfowl, like this one dating from his Cambridge days, were in watercolour. The picture was inspired by an event which he witnessed in January 1929, when the Ouse Washes were gripped by a hard frost: 'One day seven Brent Geese arrived. We could hardly believe our eyes, for the books unanimously state that the Brent never crosses high-tide mark. But here were these fine white-bellied ones, 40 miles from the sea.'

4. Self-portrait skating

c. 1930

Pencil, watercolour and bodycolour 7³⁄₁₆ × 10³⁄₈
(18.2 × 26.4)
Private collection

In his autobiography Peter wrote of the joys of skating:

> But the best part of skating was the thing itself – the magic of the swift movement over the ice. There was pure physical enjoyment in the speed and the power, the steepness of the curves in a spiral, the neatness of a grape-vine, the freedom of a high three-jump: it was fast and glossy as silk. There was also pair-formation.
>
> In birds pair-formation usually involves a ritualised display of some complexity. In the human species it is no less complex, and the display on ice was no less ritualised. My comparative skill in waltzing and the Ten Step ensured for me an array of charming partners of varying degrees of skill and beauty.

5. Sketchbook

early to mid-1930s

Pencil, sheet size 5 × 7 (12.8 × 17.8)
Private collection

This small sketchbook, which dates from Peter's early years at the East Lighthouse, Sutton Bridge, was used by him to experiment with ideas for compositions before beginning a painting.

PETER SCOTT
Yachtsman and Wildfowler

by JOHN WINTER

Sky and water have always played a very important part in Peter Scott's life; indeed rumour has it that he could swim before he could walk. It is to his keen observation of both of these, just as much as of the birds, that his pictures owe so much.

I have been privileged to share many hours and days afloat with him both as a yachtsman and a wildfowler and at both he was a master. At Cambridge we had met in the sailing world and been attracted into the International 14ft Dinghy Class by Stewart Morris, surely the all-time champion of dinghy sailors, and by Uffa Fox, unique among small boat designers, both of whom were to play such important parts in our sailing lives for the next twenty years.

For some years Peter and I were keen rivals, each with his own boat competing for the coveted Prince of Wales Cup, the championship of the 14ft

class. We were also on a number of occasions both members of successful UK teams against Canadian and US 14-footers, including a delightful visit to Lake Ontario in 1934 with our boats and with Uffa Fox as our team manager. And then at Lowestoft in 1937, Peter won the Prince of Wales Cup for the first time in *Thunder* beating me in *Lightning* by 16 seconds in an exciting finish. Since I had myself won it in *Lightning* in 1934, we decided that the time had come to join forces.

Uffa Fox built *Thunder and Lightning* for us in 1938, incorporating our joint ideas for the perfect boat. With her we won the Prince of Wales Cup together at Falmouth in 1938 using for the first time on any racing dinghy a trapeze wire to support the crew outboard. The trapeze was thereafter banned in the class for some thirty years but then reintroduced, and it is now allowed for both crew and helmsman.

After the war we again won the Cup with *Thunder and Lightning* at Brixham in 1946 and, though thereafter able to give less and less time to it, we had a number of other successes with her over the next ten years. Although the 14-footer was Peter's first love, his yachting successes were by no means confined to that class. In 1936 he was chosen to represent Great Britain in single-handed sailing in the Olympic Games at Kiel when he won the Bronze Medal and very nearly the Silver, a remarkable achievement in a class of boat in which he had little experience as we had none in this country. And then in 1964 after a series of trials, he was selected as helmsman of *Sovereign*, our chal-

Left
John Winter (above) and Peter in International 14ft dinghy *Thunder and Lightning*

lenger for the America's Cup that year against the USA's *Constellation* at Newport, Rhode Island. Although he was no more successful than many other British challengers in over a century, it was a remarkable achievement for a dinghy sailor with very little experience of sailing larger boats to win selection, and knowing Peter I have no doubt that had *Sovereign* been as close winded in her design as *Constellation*, he could have been successful.

On the administrative side of yachting, Peter also played a major part. After the war we served together on the Council of the Yacht Racing Association (now the RYA) and on its Dinghy Committee. As Chairman of the Olympic Yachting Committee he organised the successful Olympic Yachting Regatta in 1948 at Torquay and from 1964–9 he was President of the International Yacht Racing Union, the body responsible for world yachting, a position in which his tact, charm and experience were invaluable.

While sailing occupied most of our spare time before the war in the summer, wildfowling did so in the winter and in particular punt gunning to which I was introduced by Peter from his Lighthouse home on the Wash soon after we first met. Only those who have done it can understand the fascination and challenge in stalking a flock of ducks or geese at sea lying concealed in a 22ft long two-man boat drawing only a few inches of water and propelled through the shallows by pushing with 'setting' poles to within a 60yd range of the quarry without disturbing them. Though the objective was to make a successful shot, which

Peter and his wife Philippa
watching the Olympic yacht
racing regatta as Chairman of
the Jury, Tokyo, 1964

itself required skill, the art and excitement was in the stalk.

As well as to the Wash our punting expeditions together often took us to the estuaries of Morecambe Bay, the Solway, the Ribble and on one occasion to Strangford Lough and Lough Foyle in Northern Ireland. During one extremely frosty moonlit night at sea on Lough Foyle we had the excitement of catching alive a winged White-fronted Goose, which by the yellow colour of its bill was to help in establishing that the White-fronted Geese that winter in Ireland come from

15

breeding grounds in West Greenland. This in turn eventually led to its recognition as a separate race from the more usual pink-billed birds breeding in north-east Russia and Siberia.

Depending on tides, a day's punting could begin before dawn, often with no opportunity of returning before dusk, and it was a wonderful opportunity to observe the birds and wildlife of an estuary at very close quarters. It was also a wonderful way to get to know the character of one's companion.

Left
Peter punt gunning on
Wigtown Bay

NOTE: *Thunder and Lightning* was handed over to the National Maritime Museum by Peter and John on 10 June 1989.

17

2 A PROFESSIONAL ARTIST

Where the River Nene runs out into the Wash, just east of Sutton Bridge in Lincolnshire, stand two lighthouses which were built in the eighteenth century to commemorate the drainage of the Great Fens. The buildings had been well known landmarks to Peter and his wildfowling friends since 1930 when they first discovered Terrington Marsh, the stretch of salting lying between the river and King's Lynn. In 1933 Peter rented the disused East Lighthouse and made it his home until the outbreak of the Second World War. It had four storeys and one room per floor, each room with slanting curved walls so that the top room was just 6ft in diameter. The floor below was his bedroom and beneath this was a room with two beds which could be lowered from the ceiling by block and tackle. In due course Peter added an entrance porch, a studio, a bunk room and a garage, and he appointed Kenzie Thorpe, a local poacher, to look after his tame waterfowl.

In the 1930s the spring tides surrounded the Lighthouse on three sides, making it a suitable place to keep a collection of wildfowl. The first enclosure was very small but the next one covered three acres of salting. Many of the birds were

The East Lighthouse at Sutton Bridge where the Nene runs into the Wash, *c.* 1935

pinioned so that they could not fly away, and these in turn attracted wild geese and ducks which took advantage of the good facilities and made their home at the Lighthouse. By 1938 Peter had two hundred birds altogether, including many kinds of duck and twenty-five different types of geese. There were both British birds and foreign ones, including rarities such as the Red-breasted Goose, the Emperor Goose and the *Cereopsis*. Living amongst the birds he was able to study closely their appearance and behaviour and put this knowledge to good use in his paintings and books, lectures and broadcasts. He was fascinated particu-

19

larly by the way wild geese form a permanent pair bond and keep their young with them until the breeding season comes round again.

The birds were treated as individuals and many were given names. Anabel was a young Pink-footed Goose who first came to the Lighthouse in September 1936. On arrival she was not given a friendly greeting by the tame Pinkfeet, but she had probably never seen a human being before and passed within twenty yards of Peter. After a week she was quite tame and she then spent the winter at the Lighthouse. In the following May she departed on migration, two months after the big flocks had left, only to return again the following autumn. She walked straight up to her foster parent, who subsequently wrote:

> I suppose the return of Anabel on that October morning was one of the half-dozen most stirring events that I have ever experienced.

After spending another winter at the Lighthouse Anabel departed in May 1938 and sadly did not return. Her story was made known to thousands at the time through broadcasts made by Peter and his friend Michael Bratby.

To paint wildlife successfully requires specialist knowledge, not just of the animals but also of their habitats. It also presents its special problems: unlike people animals do not remain stationary for any length of time. Birds in flight present a particularly difficult subject and prior to the 1930s had been painted realistically by only a very few artists.

One such man was Frank Southgate, who lived in Norfolk and died during the First World War. Like Peter he was a wildfowler and knew his quarry intimately, and some of his compositions greatly inspired the young man. But Southgate was primarily a watercolourist, while Peter wanted to work only in oils and on a large scale. He wrote of his aims:

> I had only to put on to the canvas, to the best of my oil painting capacity, the birds as I had seen them at dawn or dusk or moonlight, or in storm or frost or snow, and I could not fail to be doing something original. It remained to be seen whether those who looked at the pictures would be moved in the same way as I was when I watched the flight of the wild geese, and heard their music.

In order to capture the tense excitement he felt on the marshes and mudflats Peter painted from memory and very quickly, having several canvases in progress at a given moment (once, in order to finish a large commission on time, he had to enlist the services of his mother to help paint some tall reeds). Lingering too long on a picture meant that the immediacy of the original inspiration was lost. He often worked all day and long into the night, lighting his easel with a pair of Aladdin lamps. He was brimming over with ideas and did not find it difficult to produce forty pictures in a few months, as he did prior to his first London exhibition in 1933. The show was a success and was followed by

International 14ft dinghy
Eastlight being sailed by Peter
and crewed by Nicholas
Cooke, *c.* 1934

regular exhibitions before and after the War, each one opened by a famous person. Royal visitors came, including Princess Elizabeth and the Queen (H.M. Queen Elizabeth the Queen Mother), the latter buying a picture of Pink-footed Geese against a sunset (No. 40).

Country Life had already published several of Peter's articles and in 1935 they published his first book, *Morning Flight*. Together with *Wild Chorus*, produced three years later, this book is now regarded as one of the classic accounts of wildfowl and wildfowling. The two volumes were illustrated with many black-and-white and colour plates of his paintings, and the text was punctuated with exquisite line drawings. The success of the books led to regular illustrative work and writing in the years to come and established Peter's name with a broad consensus of people. The limited edition prints which were produced from some of his pictures also proved very popular with lovers of the countryside and wildlife.

In the spring of 1936 Peter went to the plains of Hungary as special correspondent for *The Field* and saw geese in really big numbers for the first time. In that one area there were at least 100,000 birds. Although he failed to catch any Red-breasted Geese he brought back other birds for the Lighthouse collection and was henceforth a committed traveller. He returned to Hungary six months later and was given a very warm welcome by the gypsies who played music and composed a song about 'Scott Peter' and his search for 'red-necked geese'. At the end of this trip he returned home accompanied by fifteen geese in three crates but because of fog, was unable to fly beyond Erfurt in Germany, and only just made the train to the Hook of Holland. The birds were still with him but he had left behind all his luggage and money.

In November 1937 Peter continued his search for large flocks of Red-breasted Geese with a journey to Persia and the Caspian Sea, where he learned how to catch ducks with a flare, gong and net. This unusual skill was performed under total darkness in two boats, one with a man in the stern beating a gong, and another with a flare in the bow shielded by a hood, behind which stood a man with a large net. When the startled ducks took to wing they were caught with an adroit sweep of the net. The people here were hospitable but Peter was surprised to find he had no furniture in his room, as sitting, eating and sleeping were all done at floor level!

A year later Peter travelled to Toronto as captain of an International 14ft dinghy team and took the opportunity afterwards to visit the Gun Club at Cap Tourmente in Canada. The Club building was situated in the feeding grounds of the geese, and on one occasion was totally surrounded by a flock of four or five thousand Greater Snow Geese – then almost the entire world population of these birds. Peter's photographs of the spectacle appeared in *Life*, and the large picture window at the Club which looked out on the birds later inspired his studio window at Slimbridge.

In the decade before the War sailing, next to wildfowling, was the recreation which gave Peter

Peter sailing *Eastlight*
International 14ft dinghy
designed and built by Uffa
Fox

most pleasure. At Cambridge he had joined the University sailing club, where he had met Stewart Morris, an accomplished sailor with whom he started a friendly rivalry. During holidays on the Broads he was usually Stewart's crew in a 14ft dinghy, but soon he was competent enough to take the helm of his own boat. In 1933 he commissioned the first of a series of dinghies from Uffa Fox, one of the greatest designers of small boats this century, and wrote of the pleasures of sailing them:

> Sailing a 14ft dinghy . . . was utterly satisfying. I enjoyed it most in a breeze of wind. Beating to windward I sat on the gunwale, shoulder to shoulder with my crew. With our toes tucked under a special strap we both leant out as far as we could to bring the boat upright, trying to counteract the heeling moment of the wind. . . .

It was to lead him to a number of successes. The following year Peter went to Canada as a member of the British sailing team, and in 1936 he won the bronze medal for single-handed sailing at that year's Olympic Games. His great ambition, however, was to win the Prince of Wales Cup, the most prestigious race for 14ft dinghies. This he did for the first time in a new dinghy, *Thunder*, in 1937, followed by further wins with John Winter in 1938 and 1946 with *Thunder and Lightning*.

Catalogue

6. Self-portrait

1933

Oil painting 24 × 24 (61 × 61)
Private collection

The image presented is very much that of the serious wildfowler, with gun, cartridge belt and waders. The picture was used as the frontispiece in Peter's first book, *Morning Flight*, when it was published in 1935.

7. Pinkfeet in huge skeins fly from Holkham Fresh Marsh at dusk

1933

Oil painting 15 × 20 (37.9 × 50.5)
Tyson Jackson

The private fresh marsh at Holkham adjoining Wells-next-the-Sea in Norfolk was frequented each winter by several thousand Pink-footed Geese. They fed there during the day and flew out at night to Stiffkey high-sand, a stretch of salting lying to the east.

8. John Winter sailing *Lightning*

1934

Oil painting 24 × 24 (61 × 61)
Private collection

The occasion depicted is the Prince of Wales Cup
at Lowestoft in 1933 when John Winter was
crewed by Beecher Moore. A highly skilled
helmsman, John won the Prince of Wales Cup in
Lightning in 1934 and came second in 1935, 1936
and 1937, on the latter occasion being beaten by
Peter sailing *Thunder*. Subsequently they sailed
together in a new boat, *Thunder and Lightning*, in
1938 and again after the war in 1946, winning on
both occasions.

9.   Portrait of John Winter

c. 1940

Pencil drawing 8³⁄₁₆ × 5³⁄₁₆ (20.8 × 13.2)
Private collection

10.   Mallards rising at dawn from a pool on the salting

1934

Oil painting 22 × 40 (55.5 × 101.8)
Colonel G.A. Murray-Smith

The Mallards which come to our shores in
winter are much more wary and unapproachable
than those that breed here. In Norfolk and
Lincolnshire they congregate in large numbers on
the mudflats where they roost during the day,
flying inland at night to feed on the potato fields
and drink and preen in pools. This picture was
exhibited in the artist's second London exhibition
in 1934 and was produced shortly afterwards as a

limited edition print. A variant of the picture with a slightly different arrangement of birds was painted to commission.

11, 12. Portrait studies of Elizabeth Bergner

c. 1934

Pencil drawings, each 10 × 7 (25.3 × 17.9)
Private collection

Peter met Elizabeth Bergner when she was playing the part of the young waif Gemma Jones in Margaret Kennedy's play *Escape Me Never*. He was so taken by her performance that he took his godfather, Sir James Barrie, to see the play and introduced him to her afterwards. They became friends and the theme of Barrie's last play, *The Boy David*, seems to have come from her.

13. Swans flying

c. 1935

Brush and ink and Chinese white 7 × 9 (17.8 × 22.9)
Private collection

This drawing and number 14 were produced as text illustrations for *Morning Flight*. The ordinary edition of the book contained altogether 46 black-and-white plates, 16 colour plates and 9 line drawings, but the deluxe limited edition of 1935 had some additional illustrations.

14. Barnacle Geese

1933

Brush and ink 14½ × 10 (36.8 × 25.4)
Private collection

15. Tufted Drakes diving

1935

Oil painting 15 × 18 (38.1 × 45.7)
Private collection

The disturbed water around the bird in the foreground indicates that it has just come up from a dive, while the other two birds are probably about to go down. The vigorous palette knife technique helps to convey the activity of the scene.

16. Pinkfeet migrate high

1935

Oil painting 24 × 24 (61 × 61)
Private collection

Three years after this was painted the artist wrote of the mysteries of migration in *Wild Chorus*:

> I do not think that sight is a factor in a migratory bird's sense of direction. Experiments seem to show more and more that there is something to which birds are sensitive and we are not. It has been suggested that this something is the earth's magnetic field. . . .
>
> Whatever may be the scientific explanation of these things, the migration of birds will remain for me one of the world's supreme wonders. . . .

17. Portrait of the Duke of York (later King George VI)

1935

Pencil 9¹⁵⁄₁₆ × 7⅞ (25.2 × 18.7)
Private collection

In 1935 the Duke of York came to Leinster Corner to sit for Peter's mother who modelled two busts of him. Peter took the opportunity to make this quick pencil portrait.

18. 'It is the nightingale's frog-voice that distinguishes him'

c. 1936

Pen, brush and ink 4⁵⁄₁₆ × 3¹⁵⁄₁₆ (11 × 10)
Elizabeth Jane Howard

This drawing, together with numbers 19 and 20, was amongst those produced as illustrations for *A Bird in the Bush*, which was written by Peter's stepfather, Lord Kennet, and published in 1936.

19. 'The innocent had the manner of one who performs a duty'

c. 1936

Brush and ink 4³⁄₁₆ × 3³⁄₁₆ (10.6 × 8.1)
Elizabeth Jane Howard

20. 'The Whitethroat gives himself no airs'

c. 1936

Pen, brush and ink 4¼ × 5¼ (10.7 × 13.4)
Elizabeth Jane Howard

21. The East Lighthouse, Sutton Bridge

1937

Oil painting 20 × 30 (50.8 × 76.2)
Private collection

22. Golden Eagle

1937

Oil painting 24 × 24 (61 × 61)
Private collection

23. The coming of winter on the Danube Delta

1938

Oil painting 40 × 60 (101.6 × 152.4)
Christopher J. Fox

This picture was occasioned by a visit to Hungary in the autumn of 1936 with the purpose of finding and catching Red-breasted Geese. Not finding any there, Peter journeyed on through

Romania to the Black Sea and the Danube Delta, arriving at the same time as a blizzard. The Continental winter had driven most of the geese further south and he only saw a few thousand White-fronted and Greylag Geese and 14 Redbreasts.

24. Lesser White-fronted Geese flighting over the Caspian Marshes at dawn

1947

Oil painting 20 × 30 (49.5 × 74.9)
Private collection

This view of rare Lesser White-fronted Geese against the snow-capped Elburz mountains recalls a visit to Persia and the Caspian Sea in 1937. Here, after hunting for a week, Peter discovered a lagoon where all the Caspian Lesser White-fronts collected in mid-winter. For him they were 'exquisite and delicate little birds, with . . . golden ringed eyes, . . . tiny pink bills and smart white foreheads, . . . brilliant orange legs and black barred tummies.'

25. Barnacle Geese

1938

Oil painting 24 × 24 (61 × 61)
Private collection

26. Barnacle Geese against a stormy sky

1939

Oil painting 36 × 96 (91.4 × 243.8)
Private collection

For its date this must be one of the most
monumentally large pictures of birds painted. It
is one of a number of huge compositions which
the artist submitted to the Royal Academy
Summer Show each year. He devised the format
partly because he liked working on a large scale,
but also because it meant the pictures would
have a good chance of being hung at the RA
above the famous 'line', in other words just
below ceiling level. In the exhibition the
sensation of looking up at the painted geese and
the background skyscape must have been very
similar to that of seeing wild geese flying
overhead.

PETER SCOTT
Wildlife Preservation

by GERALD DURRELL

There is only one way to describe Peter, and that is to say that he is a magical man with skills that would have made Merlin envious. Apart from anything else, how he can continue to look so young at eighty – almost as young as when I first met him forty years ago – is not only miraculous but a source of bitter envy to the likes of us who have grown circular and grey in the cause of conservation.

I think it is his enthusiasm that is his most endearing quality – a bubbling enthusiasm which it is so easy to lose when one gets older.

I remember going down to see him at Slimbridge when he had first obtained the property. Ostensibly I went to see my friend, John Yealland, who was then curator there, for John and I were planning a collecting trip to West Africa, but at the same time I wanted to see what Peter was up to as

The studio window at
Slimbridge in the late 1950s

it sounded suspiciously like an idea I was formulating to found my Wildlife Preservation Trust in Jersey.

Peter showed me round with great ebullience, pointing out soggy field after soggy field and describing in glowing terms what he intended to do with them. Privately, I vouchsafed my view to John Yealland that I thought Peter was mad. The idea of the Trust was an excellent one, but the place I thought impossible. Who, I wanted to know, was going to go to the back of beyond to stand up to their ankles in freezing water? No one.

Well, fortunately I was wrong, for most of the British Isles, to say nothing of people all over the world, apparently were just waiting for the chance to do just that, and Slimbridge today is the huge success it deserves to be. If nothing else, this experience taught me I could be wrong. Years later Peter gave enormous help and advice to my own fledgling organisation when it started and became, indeed, our first scientific advisor. He did not at any point in time tell me I was mad.

Some years after the foundation of Slimbridge, I was going collecting to South America and I went down to see Peter to ask if there were any ducks or geese I could get him. Over lunch, he talked at great length about Torrent Ducks and it was obvious that he would not be satisfied until he possessed some. He waxed lyrical about their beauty and their extraordinary habits and said that I must get him some at all costs. Philippa had remained silent during this panegyric about Torrent Ducks, but now she felt constrained to speak.

'But Peter, that's all very well, but where are we going to *keep* them?' she asked, sensibly enough.

Peter looked at her in amazement. 'Why, build a torrent for them, of course,' he said, surprised that Philippa should not have thought of this simple solution for herself.

'But where's the money coming from?' persisted Philippa.

'Money?' said Peter, as if his wife had uttered an unladylike expletive. 'Money? Oh, we'll soon get money for a *torrent*.'

He said it with such conviction that I had a vivid

54. Mandarin Ducks, 1949 (p. 73)

66. The Natural World of Man, 1963 (p. 112)

mental picture of huge queues of millionaires forming, cheque books at the ready, panting to invest in a torrent. We need a lot more of this sort of positive thinking in conservation.

Peter during his multi-faceted lifetime has probably done more for world conservation than any other one man. We who have worked in conservation over the years are proud to send birthday greetings to one who has inspired us in so many ways. To be born with all Peter's gifts is a wonderful thing; what is even more wonderful is the way he has managed to share these gifts with so many people all over the world.

3 WAR YEARS

In the period just before the outbreak of the Second
World War Peter found alternative homes for the
birds at the Lighthouse. Some went to Walcot Hall
and others into the care of friends on Holbeach
Marsh and Horsey Island. Early in 1939 his yachting experience qualified him for the Royal Naval
Volunteer Supplementary Reserve, and as soon as
war was declared in September he was called up.
He hoped for a destroyer appointment. He
attended destroyer courses at Plymouth but was
prevented from joining HMS *Acasta* because of a
bad cold and bronchitis. A few weeks later the ship
was sunk with the loss of all her officers.

From 1940–2 Peter served as a Lieutenant in
HMS *Broke*, an old destroyer which became his
pride and joy for she was involved first in the
Battle of France and later in the Battle of the
Atlantic. Initially he suffered from seasickness, so
had a spell of leave with his family during which he
met the girl he was to fall in love with and marry in
1942, Elizabeth Jane Howard. On returning to his
ship he helped after the fall of Dunkirk in the
evacuation of troops from St Valéry and Brest. As
embarkation officer he saw to the removal of
ninety-five wounded men from St Valéry and
expected that more could be got away, but the ship
was ordered back to Portsmouth and in spite of

HMS *Broke* in which Peter
served for two years

protests nothing could be done to prevent those remaining being taken prisoner.

Towards the end of 1940 Peter was promoted to First Lieutenant and camouflaged his ship according to a new scheme he had devised. The aim was to make the ship less visible at night to U-boats on the surface, and this could be achieved if she was painted as pale as possible. A dark destroyer always stands out in silhouette against the sky at night, but a pale one would be nearly the same colour as the brightness above the horizon. The whites, pale blues and greys of *Broke* soon spread to most other ships in the Atlantic, and the scheme was so successful that vessels occasionally collided without having noticed each other.

Once France had been overrun, *Broke* was put on convoy escort duty in the Atlantic and had to brave the heavy seas of winter and the threat of attack by U-boats. In April 1941 the ship went to the rescue of HMS *Comorin*, an armed merchant cruiser which had caught fire in a north Atlantic gale. The waves were 60ft high and the only way to carry out the rescue was to go alongside so that the men could jump onto *Broke's* deck. The ships pounded together and while the deck of one was rising that of the other was falling at incredible speed, but in spite of this there were only 25 hospital cases out of the 180 rescued. Afterwards *Broke's* Captain, Bryan Scurfield, was awarded the OBE for his magnificent seamanship and Peter was Mentioned in Despatches.

After two years with *Broke* Peter was hoping to be put in command of a destroyer. The Admiralty, however, had other plans for him and early in 1942 he accepted command of a new Steam Gunboat (SGB 9, later re-named *Grey Goose*). Within a year he became Senior Officer of a flotilla of six of these ships, each of which was 150ft long and had a crew of forty. Their job and that of the Coastal Forces generally was to regain control of the English Channel after France had fallen into enemy hands. Peter summed up the struggle in his book *The Battle of the Narrow Seas*:

For more than four years a battle went on to

prevent the Germans from using coastwise shipping to relieve their roads and railways and, at
the same time, to keep open our own convoy
routes round the southern and eastern shores of
England. A large part in this battle was played
by our . . . Coastal Forces. They fought in these
waters, mostly at night, against enemy convoys
and their escorts over on the other side and
against E-boats which came across this side to
attack our convoys.

In August 1942 SGB 9 took part in the Dieppe
Raid, a surprise night attack of ships, aeroplanes
and infantry in which she was to support landings
on two beaches. The boat had just completed her
trials and this was her first spell of action, during
which she came under attack from shore batteries
and was temporarily disabled by dive-bombers.
Peter was very pleased with the way the ship and
its crew performed and had no regrets at leaving
the world of destroyers.

Early the following year Peter's first child
Nicola was born. For several months his ship was
in the dockyard having bigger guns fitted, but
when she was ready for sea again a summer of
grim fighting began in the Channel which he
described as 'perhaps the most hazardous and
certainly the most nerve-shredding part of my
life'. On the night of 16 April, for instance, he took
three ships to patrol in the Baie de la Seine and
fought a battle with three heavily armed trawlers.
In the action one of the Motor Gunboats ran out of
ammunition and the steering gear of the Steam

Gunboat was shot away. After hand-steering had been rigged two ships were able to pursue the trawlers, one of which was hit, set on fire and stopped. Peter, now a Lieutenant-Commander, was considered to have shown 'great determination in his engagement, pursuit and re-engagement of the enemy' and was awarded the Distinguished Service Cross.

For the last two years of the war Peter was diverted to the planning side, at first at Portsmouth Combined Headquarters where his office was in 'The Tunnel', a series of mine-like galleries cut out of the chalk of Portsdown Hill. Here he and Christopher Dreyer were responsible for the planning of all Coastal Forces to be used in the Normandy invasion. In the Naval Plotting Room the positions of enemy ships were detected by radar and marked on a huge map of the Channel, so that it was possible for the Controlling Officer to make the interception calculations and radio these to his ships. The technique was successful up to a range of 25–30 miles, but the sea lane along which the bulk of the shipping would pass during the invasion was to be 70 miles long. To control the Coastal Forces which would be protecting the sea lane Peter and Christopher deployed a new technique in naval warfare. Four frigates were equipped with radars and Control Officers appointed to each, who watched the movements of the smaller ships on the Cathode Ray Tube and directed the battle. The frigates had to be stationed within 5 miles of the scene of action.

During D-Day and the establishment of the

Normandy Bridgehead the technique proved highly successful. Shortly afterwards Peter went to France and spent most of the next two months there, establishing a radar plot in a dugout and planning operations for the Motor Torpedo Boats operating out of Courseulles and Cherbourg. He summed up the situation in a notebook he kept at the time:

> In July 1944 the Allied bridgehead is, as it were, an island surrounded by the war – an incredible Alice-in-Wonderland island. Along the landward perimeter is the front line with the din of artillery bombardment and the frightful destruction of towns and villages. Along the seaward side is the war of E-boats [Enemy War Motorboats] and mine-laying aircraft and the destruction from the D-day landings.

By late August 1944 no targets remained for the Coastal Forces west of the Straits of Dover. There were operations to be directed against German evacuation convoys off the Dutch coast, but as usual the winter campaign was governed largely by the weather. In October Peter was sent to a Prisoner-of-War Camp to interview 'Charlie' Müller, a Senior Officer of the Tenth Schnellboot Flotilla who was a renowned E-boat Commander. He had been told that as Charlie was a prisoner for the duration of the war he could tell him any secrets that might lead to secrets in return. So they had frank discussions about the war and the actions in which they had fought against each other, and

Peter showed Charlie the manuscript of a book he was writing on the Coastal Forces (*Battle of the Narrow Seas*). The German later profited unexpectedly from the discussions when he was returned to Germany by mistake from a transit camp in the United States, in exchange for a well-known politician. After his release a large number of E-boats simultaneously attacked the East Convoy Route, greatly confusing the radar – a line of attack which had been put to 'Charlie' as a possibility at the interview.

In the spring of 1945 Peter was offered the command of *Cardigan Bay*, a new anti-aircraft frigate which was just being completed. The war ended before the ship was commissioned and on 13 May he went to meet surrendering E-boats off the Thames estuary. Later Peter was one of the BBC commentators for the victory procession but words failed him when it came to describing the strange pagoda-like erection in Parliament Square. On the following day the *Times* drew attention to his description! Since then he has never enjoyed doing running commentaries for radio or television, except on subjects with which he is very familiar.

Peter had not previously entertained the idea of a career in politics, but with his war record and the example of his step-father to look up to, he was in many ways a suitable candidate. In July 1945 the Chairman of the Conservative Association of Rugby asked him to join the short-list of prospective candidates to stand as MP for Rugby in the general election. He was not selected there but became the Conservative candidate for Wembley North, and with only two weeks in which to make himself known to the electorate he threw himself into the speech-making and campaigning. He failed to get in by 435 votes.

Catalogue

27. Portrait of Jane Howard

1940

Pencil 13¼ × 9⁹⁄₁₆ (33.8 × 23.1)
Robin Howard

28. Portrait of Wayland Young

1940

Pencil 12⅝ × 8½ (32.3 × 21.5)
Private collection

The sitter is Peter's step-brother, now Lord Kennet.

29. Wigeon crossing low over the creek

1942

Oil painting 16 × 24 (40.6 × 70)
Private collection

30. Portrait of Jane

1942

Pen and ink 9¹⁵⁄₁₆ × 8³⁄₁₆ (25.2 × 20.8)
Elizabeth Jane Howard

A few months after Peter and Jane Howard were married they stayed at Cowes while his new Steam Gun Boat was being commissioned. He made several drawings of her, mostly in ink, and wrote of them later: 'The ink line was simple and uncompromising. It had to be right the first time. These were probably the best portrait drawings I have made in all my life. Drawing was an urgent and essential escape to a creative life.'

31. Portrait of Nicola Scott, eleven days old

1943

Pencil 7 × 5¼ (17.7 × 13.2)
Elizabeth Jane Howard

In *The Eye of the Wind* Peter wrote that 'our daughter Nicola was born in a nursing home in Kensington, 10 days earlier than she was expected. At 11 days old, the day on which she and her mother returned to Clifton Hill, I made my first drawing of her, the first of many. I was a proud and wondering father, proudest perhaps of my young wife.'

32. Moonlight attack

1943

Oil painting 18 × 22 (45.7 × 55.9)
Private collection

This picture of a 70ft Motor Torpedo Boat in

action was used as the frontispiece illustration in Peter's book *The Battle of the Narrow Seas*, which was published in 1945.

33.   Portrait of Lieutenant Commander R.P. Hichens

1948

Oil painting 24 × 36 (61 × 91.4)
RNVR Officers' Association

In the 1930s Peter's friend Robert Hichens sailed 14ft dinghies and was a regular contender for the Prince of Wales Cup. During the war he won many decorations serving in Coastal Forces but was tragically killed by a stray shell at the end of a successful battle in April 1943. After hearing the news Peter gave a broadcast about the Coastal Forces and made 'Hitch' the central theme. This proved very popular and even made headlines in the daily press. After the War Peter was commissioned to paint a portrait of his friend relying on memory and a few photographs.

34.   Portrait of Colin Howard

1944

Pencil 7¾ × 6⅝ (19.8 × 16.8)
Elizabeth Jane Howard

The artist's brother-in-law.

35. House Sparrows at a bird table

1944

Pen and ink 6 × 10 (15.1 × 25.3)
Private collection

36. Black-tailed Godwit

1944

Pen, brush and ink 5⅝ × 7⅝ (14.2 × 19.3)
Private collection

37. The alert

1944

Pen, brush and ink 6⅛ × 9⅞ (15.6 × 25.1)
Private collection

The subject is a Heron and a pair of Mallards.

38. The Boundary Dyke in Spring

1944

Oil painting 26 × 30 (66 × 76.2)
Private collection

Shovelers are best known in England as Spring
and Winter visitors but they are also seen
regularly in Norfolk and Lincolnshire. They are
very much freshwater ducks and seldom seen at
sea. The colourful drakes make a loud drumming
noise when taking off and during display they
emit a characteristic double clucking call. When
feeding, Shovelers use their broad curiously-

shaped bills horizontally, sifting algae and floating plankton from the surface-film.

(Front cover)

39. Portrait of Nicola Scott at 22 months

1944

Pencil 10 × 7⁵⁄₁₆ (25.4 × 18.6)
Private collection

40. Pinkfeet

1945

Oil painting 20 × 30 (50.8 × 76.2)
Lent by gracious permission of HM The Queen
and HRH The Duke of Edinburgh

The geese are coming out from inland to the mudflats of the Wash at dusk. When the Queen Mother bought the picture shortly after the war she told the artist she had often seen Pinkfeet against such a sunset on the Wolferton marshes below Sandringham.

(Colour plate)

PETER SCOTT
Naval Service

by COMMANDER CHRISTOPHER DREYER

In the fashion which is typical of his whole life, Peter Scott managed to cram an awful lot into his naval career from late 1939, when he joined as an RNVR (Supplementary List) Sub-Lieutenant, till the summer of 1945, when he left to fight in the post-war General Election, by which time he was a Lieutenant-Commander with an MBE, two DSCs and several Mentions in Despatches.

His naval career divides into three parts – firstly, after his initial training, he served for two years in destroyers, mainly in HMS *Broke* in the Western Approaches, ending up as 1st-Lieutenant; then his time in Coastal Forces, which was mainly spent in Steam Gun Boats, ending up as Senior Officer of the Flotilla; and the final period, when he was preparing to take command of a new frigate, but left the Royal Navy at the end of the European War, when he was adopted as the Conservative candidate for Wembley North.

Peter came to us in Coastal Forces in the summer of 1942. He had been hoping to get

Right
Peter with a Lesser White-fronted Goose

52

command of a destroyer, but the Admiralty first gave him something smaller – a new Steam Gun Boat, which was being built at Cowes. SGB No. 9, which later on, when the class got names, was called *Grey Goose*, was one of these large, steel-hulled steam-driven boats, and at 150ft much bigger than the rest of our MTBs, MGBs and MLs, which together made up Coastal Forces.

Peter had *Grey Goose* for some eighteen months and for about a year he was the Senior Officer of the SGB Flotilla, mainly operating from New-haven (where my MTB Flotilla was also operating for the early part of 1943). After taking part in the Dieppe raid in August 1942, Peter and the SGBs had a number of gallant battles in the Channel in the spring and summer of 1943. The SGBs were heavily armed, but they were slow and their steam plant was vulnerable to bullets and splinters, while their large size meant that they could never make an unobserved approach. Their battles, therefore, tended to be rather formidable slogging matches, but Peter fought his boats with great bravery and determination.

When he came ashore in late 1943 he was for some months an instructor at our training base, HMS *Bee* at Holyhead, where all the newly-commissioned boats were worked up into fighting units before joining operational flotillas.

In March 1944 he joined me on the staff of Captain Coastal Forces (Channel) to prepare and operate all the Coastal Force Craft in the Channel during Operation Neptune, the naval portion of Operation Overlord, the invasion of France, which started on 6 June 1944. We had a very happy and harmonious six months together in that job: three months preparing for the invasion and three months doing it, till suddenly, early in September, we found that there were no more enemy vessels in the Channel and we had worked ourselves out of a job – all that was left was to write the report and pack up the staff.

On our small Coastal Forces Staff, attached to the C-in-C, Portsmouth, I acted as Senior Staff Officer and ran the staff and, before the invasion, Peter acted as Staff Officer Operations. Once the Operation began, Peter became a roving controller, spending some time in the assault area in France and, later on, with the Americans in Cherbourg, operating their PT boats against the Channel Islands. In between times he came back and helped us out in Portsmouth.

Peter was an invaluable staff officer, because the combination of his wide knowledge of Coastal Forces operating, his good brain and tactical sense, together with his considerable reputation, made him an excellent envoy and representative. Furthermore, he wrote most capably and his easy manner and equable temperament made it a pleasure for anyone to work with him.

Our personal friendship and agreement on principles made our own collaboration very easy. I do remember that we shared a weakness in not readily suffering fools and this did sometimes get us into trouble with our seniors around the command, some of whom had been on the Portsmouth staff since 1939 and only wanted a quiet life and a good night's sleep! Fortunately, Patrick McLaughlin, our Captain Coastal Forces, was a most pugnacious and charming man and he always rescued us when we had overstepped the mark and insulted some senior.

One of Peter's most noticeable characteristics as a sailor was his formidable determination that he must be the best at whatever he took on. When he got a command it had to be the best boat ever; when he was given a flotilla it had to be the best of the lot. I always imagined that the determination sprang from an inborn need to live up to his father's immense reputation, since he had been brought up with the background of that great sailor and explorer's heroic journeys and death.

At the same time, in parallel with his firm ambition to succeed, he was undeniably and endearingly rather scruffy – his uniforms tended to be pretty shapeless and he wore a grey cardigan underneath, which showed, and there was frequently some paint here and there, on him or his clothes.

In some respects the fact that when he joined the Royal Navy he was already a household name as a painter, author, naturalist, broadcaster and Olympic dinghy sailor, was a disadvantage to him, in that his superiors were liable to expect him to be a cocky young so-and-so and his equals were liable to be jealous. However, one soon learned that, although he neither concealed nor paraded his determination and ambition as a dedicated sailor, he was a kindly and amusing mess-mate and companion, a most excellent shipmate in any situation, and a very good friend.

4 THE WILDFOWL TRUST

Six years of war made a large gap in the lives of those who survived the armed struggle. Peter lost several very close friends and wanted nothing more than to return to his birds and his painting. In the ground floor room of his house in London he began painting hard again, but had to abandon the Lighthouse as a place to work because the sea was now half a mile away from it due to land reclamation during the war. He drew many portraits of friends, kept his diaries, wrote and illustrated books and took his pilot's licence.

In the autumn of 1945 Peter was invited to visit the Severn Estuary to look at the great flock of White-fronted Geese which wintered there. He did not think he would have time, but by a strange coincidence a letter arrived from his old friend Will Tinsley which was to change his mind. Will told him that a few years ago a wild Lesser White-fronted Goose had joined the tame ones at his house. At that time the Lesser White-front had been recorded only once before in Britain, but it was very difficult to distinguish from the ordinary White-front and Peter wondered if odd birds of the rare species might occasionally join flocks of the common one on migration and thus make their

The Honorary Director's house (now Curator's house), at Slimbridge *c.* 1947

way to Britain. He decided to put his theory to the test with a visit to Slimbridge and was delighted to spot two Lesser White-fronts along with six other species of goose. The concentration of wildfowl was fabulous and, in his own words,

> as we walked back . . . I came to the inescapable conclusion that this was the place in which anyone who loved wild geese must live. Here were two empty cottages which might become the headquarters of the research organisation which had been taking shape in my mind over the years, the headquarters of a new collection of waterfowl, of the scientific and educational effort which I believed was so badly needed for

Very early sea wall hide,
Slimbridge

the conservation of wildfowl . . . I looked at my surroundings with a new eye, an eye to the future, for this was the beginning of the Wildfowl Trust.

At Slimbridge the main feeding ground of the geese lies between the Gloucester and Berkeley Canal and the tidal shore in an area of reclaimed land known as the New Grounds. It was clear that the sea wall, which keeps the spring tides out of the fields, would provide ideal opportunities for approaching the wildfowl unobserved. In the summer of 1946 the first observation huts were built along the wall by German prisoners-of-war. These had benches, hinged shutters and covered

59

Early hide made from a
cladding of reeds, Slimbridge

approaches and were the prototypes of many hides
built elsewhere. Also in that first year the 100-
year-old duck decoy was restored, ponds were dug
out around the old farm cottage and a fox-proof
fence was put up. The first enclosure was prepared
for the arrival of the nucleus of the tame wildfowl
collection – fifty birds assembled by Gavin Max-
well. However, when the birds arrived the new
pen was not quite finished and they had to spend
their first night at Slimbridge in an empty bun-
galow. Otherwise there were no hiccups and two

years later the collection of birds had grown to 400 individuals representing 67 species.

On 10 November 1946 a meeting was held to agree to form a new educational charity, the Severn Wildfowl Trust (the 'Severn' was dropped from the title in 1955), and in the aims of the organisation were to be research, education, conservation and recreation; and visitors would be able to walk among the tame wildfowl in the enclosure or observe the wild flocks from the hides. Field-Marshal Lord Alanbrooke became the Trust's first President and from the outset devoted much of his time to it. John Yealland was appointed to look after the collection of birds while a private secretary handled the affairs of the Trust and its Director. The first secretary left after eight months and was replaced by Philippa Talbot-Ponsonby, later to become Peter's second wife.

One of the most important tasks of the Trust in the early days was to learn about the numbers, movements and haunts of wildfowl, so that this knowledge could be used to counter the threats to the birds and their habitats. Ringing birds was one way of doing this but how could the birds be caught in the first place? Once the Slimbridge decoy was restored it could be used to catch ducks, but the goose net which Peter developed before the war needed to be updated. It occurred to him that a net could be propelled by the Schermuly Pistol Rocket Apparatus, as used for life-saving at sea. The equipment was put to the test at Slimbridge in February 1948 in the presence of A.J. Schermuly, Keith Shackleton, Philippa Talbot-Ponsonby, and a

Peter and Philippa after their marriage at the British Embassy in Rejkjavik, 1951

photographer from *Country Life*. The preparations were made in freezing-conditions before dawn and, as expected, a large flock of White-fronted Geese settled in the field where the net was set. The birds fed up to the net and thirty-two were caught. All who took part in the exercise felt it was not just a useful means of studying wildfowl but also a thrilling pastime – outwitting the geese required all the stealth and cunning of the wildfowler, but instead of being shot they were caught unharmed.

In the 1930s Peter had been impressed by the huge concentrations of ducks and geese which he saw in America, and by the steps the Americans were taking to conserve wildfowl. These included setting up many large reserves, limiting shooting to particular seasons, times of day and localities, and enforcing complete protection for endangered species. Thinking that Britain was lagging behind and could learn from the Americans, in October 1948 Peter set out on a trip to the United States and Canada. His first stop was the Delta Waterfowl Research Station near Winnipeg, where he was impressed by the incubation house, the indoor pens for rearing young birds and the large laboratory. Here he heard for the first time of X-ray examination of ducks and geese, which showed that a large proportion of them carried lead pellets in their bodies, either from shot wounds or from eating them as grit for digestion. From Delta he went on to the Bear River Marshes in Utah and the Sacramento Valley in California. The estimate of birds in the Sacramento Refuge at that time was 60,000 geese and 250,000 ducks, amongst which

An early Gazebo Tower, Slimbridge

was a flock of the rare Ross's Goose, a small white goose with black-tipped wings.

The breeding grounds of Ross's Goose had only been discovered in 1938, in the Perry River Region of Arctic Canada. When Peter decided to visit and explore this remote area in the summer of 1949 he was embarking on one of the first expeditions ever devoted to a single species of goose. His aims were to find and map the bird's breeding territory, mark as many individuals as possible, estimate the breeding population and bring back live specimens to the Wildfowl Trust. All four goals were achieved and in addition he and his colleagues made friends with the Kogmuit Eskimos.

In the early 1950s Peter made an intensive study of the Pink-footed Goose, the most abundant wild grey goose in Britain. Rocket nets were used to catch and mark samples of the population that winter in Scotland, and to further this research three expeditions were made to one of the bird's main breeding grounds, the Hofsjökul ice-cap in the central highlands of Iceland. The 1951 expedition was funded mainly by the Royal Society and the Icelandic Government and could not rely on anything more than horses for transport. During the summer there is a period when the adult geese are moulting and the young are still unable to fly, so that the entire population is flightless and can be herded together. It was found that the best way to do this was to surround several square miles of marsh with horsemen who moved the geese slowly towards a pre-arranged hill. Once assembled on the summit the birds were driven into an

Marking the catching area with feathers, rocket netting, *c.* 1950

Refurbished Berkeley New
Decoy, Slimbridge

improvised enclosure of string netting and could
be ringed and recorded, 1,000 birds being marked
in 1951 and 9,000 in 1953.

A highly important part of the conservation
work of the Wildfowl Trust has been the rearing of
endangered species in captivity. Species extinction
is, in Peter's eyes, a wicked irresponsibility which
should be averted at all costs, even if this means
capturing the last remaining wild specimens of a
particular animal. The Hawaiian Goose, or Ne-Ne,
was not quite that close to extinction but at one
time there were less than fifty individuals left alive
and it was, therefore, the rarest goose. The bird's

native territory was the jagged lava beds of Hawaii, to which it was hoped specimens bred in captivity could be reintroduced. In 1950 the Trust's curator, John Yealland, was sent to Hawaii to help with a propagation project. Two birds were sent to Slimbridge the following year. Both birds, however, made nests and laid infertile eggs, so it was clear that a male Ne-Ne was still needed!

Peter and Philippa with their children Nicola, Dafila and Falcon, and the decoy dog, Piper (a Shetland collie) in the studio. 1960

One arrived a week later but he was in full moult. However in the following season he bred with the two females and in 1952 nine young were produced. From this stock nearly 2,000 individuals have been reared to date.

For two years after the founding of the Wildfowl Trust, Peter kept his house in London and drove every weekend to Slimbridge. Gradually his centre of activity switched to Gloucestershire and in 1949 he moved into the eighteenth-century farm cottage at Slimbridge. This was a home not only for him but also his second wife Philippa, whom he married in Iceland in 1951. With their three children the cottage soon became too small and they planned a new house next door. Peter employed an architect to find practical solutions for all his ideas, not the least important of which was a spacious studio with a large picture window overlooking a pond covered with wildfowl. The new house was ready in 1954 and has been the family home ever since.

Catalogue

41. Canada Geese coming in to land

1946

Drypoint etching 9 × 14 (22.7 × 35.2)
Private collection

In 1946 Peter went to New York for an exhibition of his paintings at the Arthur Harlow Gallery. While there he executed a series of

drypoint etchings, drawing with a steel stylus directly onto copper. This print and number 42 belong to the series.

42. Mallard dropping in

1946

Drypoint etching 10 × 8 (25.2 × 20)
Private collection

43. Teal on the River Severn

1947

Oil painting 26 × 30 (66 × 76.2)
Private collection

This picture was painted a year after the
Wildfowl Trust was established on the south
bank of the River Severn at Slimbridge,
Gloucestershire. At the time Peter was still living
and painting in London, but the new estuary
landscape was already beginning to appear in his
pictures. Here it is autumn and the marsh is
flooded, while overhead a party of Teal heads
downstream, some of the birds breaking away
to land on the floodwater.

44. Emperor Geese

1947

Oil painting 26 × 30 (66 × 76.2)
Private collection

Emperor Geese live in Alaska and the Aleutian Islands. They are quite rare and, as Peter wrote in *Wild Chorus*, they 'migrate only a short distance, for the south side of the archipelago is warmed by an ocean current from Japan and in winter the geese need go no farther south to avoid the snow and ice which covers their breeding grounds on the north side.'

(Colour plate)

45. Snow Geese flying by moonlight

1947

Oil painting 10 × 14 (25.9 × 35.9)
Private collection

Many species of wildfowl are active at dawn, at dusk and during the night, and Peter has always had a special fondness for these times of day. In the 1930s many of his wildfowling expeditions took place in freezing conditions and under the cover of darkness, but by the time he painted this picture he had given up shooting. The landscape, which is imaginary, could be in north America or Canada where he had seen large flocks of Greater and Lesser Snow Geese before the War.

(Colour plate)

46. Portrait of HRH Princess Elizabeth

1947

Plasticowell 14 × 12 (35.6 × 30.4)
Private collection

In 1947 Peter was granted permission to make
portrait drawings of Princess Elizabeth and
Princess Margaret (see number 47). He went to
Buckingham Palace about half a dozen times and
drew the portraits onto plastic as lithographs
which were printed by Cowells of Ipswich. He
was afraid the drawings would not justify the
time given by the sitters, but they were pleased
with the results.

47. Portrait of HRH Princess Margaret

1947

Plasticowell 14 × 11 (35.5 × 27.9)
Private collection

48. Canada Geese

1948

Oil painting 12 × 16 (30.5 × 40.7)
Private collection

By the late 1940s Peter was travelling extensively
and his paintings depicted wildfowl from all over
the world, not just Britain or Europe as hitherto.
Late in 1948 he went to the United States and
saw ducks, geese and swans in great profusion,
including many Canada Geese. In this picture he

74.   Coral reef fishes, 1973 (p. 117)

77. Courtship in Loch Ness – Loch Ness Monsters, 1975 (p. 119)

has used back-lighting to enhance the tonal contrasts and produce a more atmospheric effect. It is a device which he has used in many of his paintings and still favours today.

49. American Green-winged Teal at sunset

1948

Oil painting 10 × 14 (25.4 × 35.6)
Private collection

At the Bear River Marshes in Utah in November 1948, American Green-winged Teal could be seen in great profusion. They provided the inspiration for this picture.

50. Portrait of James Robertson-Justice

1948

Plasticowell 18½ × 12 (47 × 30.5)
Private collection

The sitter was a close friend of the artist for more than twenty years.

51. Portrait of Philippa Talbot-Ponsonby

1948

Plasticowell 14 × 12 (35.5 × 30.5)
Private collection

Peter and Philippa were married in Iceland in 1951, his first marriage having been dissolved just after the war. At the time this portrait was drawn Philippa was Peter's secretary, looking after his concerns and those of the Wildfowl Trust. Since then she has been his principal adviser and has managed his business and financial affairs. They have two children, Dafila and Falcon, who have in turn raised two and one grandchildren respectively: a daughter and a son, and a daughter.

52. Portrait of Nicola Scott

1948

Pencil 12¼ × 10 (31 × 25.5)
Mrs Nicola Starks

The daughter of Peter and Jane Howard, who
has two daughters and two sons. Currently Peter
has seven grandchildren.

53. Shelduck alighting on the Dumbles

1948

Oil painting 20 × 30 (66 × 76.3)
Private collection

The Dumbles are 200 acres of grassy saltmarsh
which lie outside the sea wall at Slimbridge. In
winter they are a feeding ground for a great flock
of White-fronted Geese and many other kinds of
waterfowl, including Wigeon, Shelduck and
Curlews.

54. Mandarin Ducks

1949

Oil painting 18 × 15 (45.7 × 37.9)
Mrs Nicola Starks

It is appropriate that Mandarin Ducks, which
look distinctly Chinese, should actually come
from China. The drakes in the picture have
raised their 'sails' – each a single scapular feather
– to a vertical position in display to the ducks.

(Colour plate)

55. Portrait of Kaota

1949

Kaota

Black and brown brush-point pens 11¾ × 9
(29.8 × 23)
Private collection

With Paul Queneau and Harold Hanson, Peter
explored the Perry River region in Arctic Canada
in the summer of 1949, during which they
mapped, filmed, collected specimens and
discovered a new breeding ground of Ross's
Goose. They also made friends with the
Kogmuit Eskimos and Kaota, a young lad, was
one of the first to come to their camp.

56. The Cranes of Jämtland

1967

Oil painting 24 × 28 (61 × 71.1)
Inherited from the late Miss Violet Maxse

This picture was commissioned by a lady
ornithologist as a souvenir of a visit which she
had made, jointly with Peter and Philippa, to
Jämtland seventeen years earlier.

57. A quiet place for Teal

1952

Oil painting 30 × 25 (76.2 × 63.5)
The Rt. Hon. Peter Walker MBE MP

Teal can be seen in their thousands at many of

the Wildfowl Trust centres in winter. The birds in this picture are resting in a quiet pool at Slimbridge. However, a sudden sound or movement would make them take wing instantly, constituting the collective noun for the species – 'a spring of Teal'.

58.   Portrait of Dafila Scott, nine days old

1952

Pencil 7⅞ × 7¹⁄₁₆ (20 × 18)
Private collection

59.   Portrait of Richard Falcon Scott, four-and-a-half days old

1954

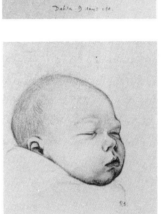

Pencil 8⅝ × 7½ (22 × 19)
Private collection

60.   Wigeon courtship

1954

Oil painting 20 × 30 (50.8 × 76.2)
Mr and Mrs Keith Shackleton

PETER SCOTT
Naturalist

by RICHARD FITTER

Polymaths are rare in the modern world, and especially polymathic naturalists. But one such is our own Peter Scott. As a naturalist too, I count myself fortunate if I find I know some fact about animals and their ways which he does not. His first love, of course, is wildfowl, but all birds are his realm, and he is also quite extraordinarily knowledgeable both on mammals and other vertebrates and on invertebrates. In fact I would classify him as the Wildlife Brain of Britain. This is perhaps less surprising when you realise how many different parts of the world he has visited, and how many radio and TV programmes he has compèred.

I have been privileged to see a great deal of Peter in various capacities, but especially when he was Chairman of two bodies with which I have been closely associated, the Fauna (now Fauna and Flora) Preservation Society and the Survival Service (now Species Survival) Commission of IUCN (International Union for Conservation of Nature).

To sit in a meeting under his efficient chairmanship was always both a pleasurable and an educational experience, for rarely does he fail to bring out some unusual anecdote or feature of animal behaviour or distribution not known to most of those present.

In the study of his chosen group, the ducks, geese and swans, he has both invented and launched many features that are now commonplace to us. He pioneered, for instance, the idea of a society devoted to the study of one group of animals, the Wildfowl and Wetlands Trust; the modern way of watching larger animals, with the aid of specially designed observation hides; the idea of an identification guide for one group of birds – his *Coloured Key to the Wildfowl of the World* appeared in 1950; and above all the use of individual markings on animals and birds in the detailed study of their movements and behaviour, with his long-term study of the Bewick's swans which visit the small lake in front of his home, making use of his own observation that every one has a slightly different bill pattern. In addition, in 1948, with C.T. Dalgety, he described the Greenland White-fronted Goose *Anser albifrons flavirostris* as a new sub-species.

One of his most fruitful ideas was the Red Data Books. These set out the facts on the current status and conservation needs of endangered species. Beginning with a volume on mammals published by IUCN in 1966, Red Data Books now cover almost all the more important animal and plant groups, on a world-wide basis, while many countries, including Britain, the USSR and China, now have Red Data Books of their own. Alas, such are the current threats to species throughout the world that Red Data Books are likely to be with us for many years yet.

Another great achievement was his fostering of the SSC's specialist groups, which has resulted in IUCN (International Union for Conservation of Nature and Natural Resources) possessing a unique world-wide network of nearly 2,000 biologists who willingly give their services for the saving of endangered species. There are now no fewer than 84 of these groups – 33 for mammals, 12 for birds (shared with ICBP (International Council for Bird Preservation) and IWRB (International Waterfowl & Wetlands Research Bureau)), 8 for lower vertebrates, 5 for invertebrates, 18 for plants and 8 interdisciplinary groups – and more are in the pipeline.

Yet among all these great achievements his major contribution remains the Wildfowl and Wetlands Trust. Nobody else had attempted to collect together in one place breeding groups of almost every extant species of a single animal group. By successfully achieving this for the ducks, geese and swans in the beautiful natural setting of the Trust's grounds on the Severn estuary, he has created a unique centre of excellence for education, research and sheer public enjoyment. This has stimulated both wide public interest and a great outburst of research into his favourite group, which continues to contribute very substantially to the knowledge needed for their survival in the modern world.

5 WRITER, RESEARCHER AND BROADCASTER

The principle of education has always been of prime importance to Peter. As a boy he was privileged to have close, almost daily, contact with animals of all sorts and in later life, realizing that not everyone is so fortunate, he has striven to give people of all ages the same opportunity. He puts the message across not only in his paintings but also in books, articles, talks, and television programmes, and gives it relevance through the live animals which can be experienced at the Wildfowl Trust centres and refuges. He believes it is best if people can be educated about nature and conservation from an early age, and the Trust has always placed much emphasis on a service to children. As a broadcaster he took regular part in *Nature Parliament* on BBC Radio's Children's Hour, which took the form of questions sent in by children and answered on the air by a panel of experts. His hosting of the *Look* television programme from 1953 to 1970 was also integral to the future development of the BBC's natural history output and enabled him to bring wildlife subjects to a wide

Peter with Eileen Moloney, Producer of *Look*, at the BBC Natural History Unit, *c.* 1962

audience. A famous example is his introduction to Heinz Sielmann's film of woodpeckers, showing them inside a tree trunk at their nest, which recorded the highest viewing figure since the coronation.

A highly curious and enquiring mind has led Peter to make a number of significant discoveries about birds and animals. The scope and nature of his interest is best explained in his own words:

I have always been deeply moved by the great diversity in animal life and the amazing ingenuity of the selective process in evolution.

How and why have all these animals become so different one from another? . . . This sense of wonder and mystery has never left me – indeed it has grown stronger as I have grown older. In the study of evolution as in all other branches of biology . . . the answer to one question prompts at least three more. It is a road which leads to the Ultimate Truth, a road along which we can travel hopefully, without ever expecting to arrive.

In 1948 Peter published a paper with Christopher Dalgety on a new race of the White-fronted Goose, giving it the Latin name *Anser albifrons flavirostris* (i.e. the goose white-fronted and yellow-billed). He discovered that this bird, which differs from the White-front wintering in England by having a yellow rather than a pink bill, breeds in Greenland and winters in Ireland. The distinguished ornithologist H.F. Witherby was sceptical about the news at first, but when he went to Peter's lighthouse on the Wash just before the war, and fed a typical pink-billed White-front from one hand and a yellow-billed Greenland bird from the other, the evidence was conclusive! Then the war intervened and it was not until 1948 that the new sub-species could be formally described to scientists.

The same year the seed was sown for another pioneering study, for this was when the first wild Bewick's Swan came to the Wildfowl Trust, on its way from Arctic Russia to winter perhaps in Ireland. By 1964 the number of birds had increased

Peter (above) and Harold Hanson in the Canadian Arctic, Perry River region, 1949

to twenty and Peter decided to attract them to the pond in front of his studio by bringing tame Whistling Swans to it. He then noticed, together with his daughter Dafila, that each individual swan has a different bill pattern, and this was the beginning of an intensive study of Bewick's Swans. In twenty-five years of research over 6,000 individuals have been recorded and named. Peter and Dafila used the discovery to find out fascinating facts about the swans' family relationships, life history, migratory routes and local movements.

The study became the subject of Dafila's PhD thesis. The work highlighted, for example, how important it is for pairs and families of swans to stay together, ensuring their health and survival in the harsh Arctic environment. Now between 300 and 400 Bewick's Swans come to Slimbridge each winter.

Peter believes that for education to be effective it must be enjoyable. For a long time he has kept a notebook in which he writes witticisms and wise sayings for use in lectures – it has not escaped his notice that an audience will be more attentive if it is wary of missing a joke! On one occasion he lectured at the Royal Institution where it is traditional that the speaker should mount the podium and start talking without any preliminaries. He came into the room and made a drawing of a Dodo on the board, for he was accustomed to use the example of its extinction to lead into the problem of conservation. He had to return twice to the drawing to make adjustments to its expression, but finally the audience could not resist laughing and the rest of the lecture went very well.

In the 1950s Peter gave many lectures to raise money for the Wildfowl Trust. He was the first person to lecture at the Royal Festival Hall in London. The subject was the 1951 Icelandic expedition, and 300 people had to be turned away. Lecture tours were also arranged, including one in the Midlands using the Trust's converted narrow boat *Beatrice* as the principal means of transport. More recently he has lectured regularly on board the *Lindblad Explorer*, the small liner which special-

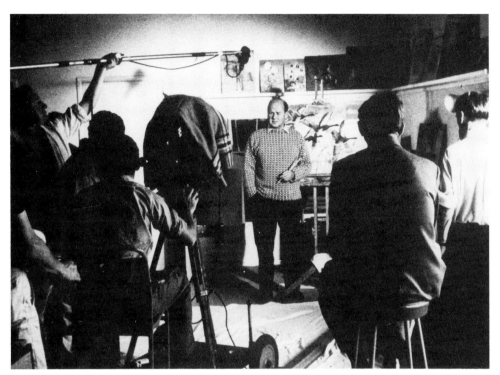

Making *Wild Wings* film,
Slimbridge

ises in sailing to remote parts of the world, and in 1979 he addressed a crowd of 12,000 people in Trafalgar Square on the whaling issue, calling for a two minute silence in honour of their plight. In spite of all this experience, however, he has never really enjoyed lecturing and still feels very nervous before going on.

Writing, on the other hand, has always been very much a part of Peter's daily life. He tends to devote diaries to specific activities such as (formerly) wildfowling, sailing, gliding and travelling, and has described himself as 'an incurable recorder'. There are over seventy volumes of his travel diaries alone, each one beautifully illustrated with pencil sketches and watercolours and inscribed with detailed notes on the wildlife he has seen. The diaries of his Perry River and Icelandic expeditions in 1949 and 1951 respectively were published by *Country Life*, and more recently excerpts from his travel diaries have been published by Collins. These show his delight not only in watching animals but also in identifying and naming them, for he always makes sure he knows the correct Latin name. The naming process is not an end in itself but merely the first stage in finding out more about wildlife, whether from comparison with similar species, observation of behaviour and distribution, or reading books.

Royal visit to Slimbridge, 1961. HM The Queen is Patron and HRH Prince Philip has served as President of the Wildfowl Trust. HRH The Prince of Wales is now President. Right to left, HRH Prince Charles, HM The Queen, Peter, HRH Prince Philip

Over the years Peter has published some sixteen books, including in 1961 his famous autobiography *The Eye of the Wind*, but he has co-written and illustrated more than twice as many again. Following in the tradition established by Roger Tory Peterson he produced plates for field guides including the *Key to the Wildfowl of the World*, first published forty years ago and still in print today, and the *Fishwatchers' guide to West Atlantic Coral Reefs*, which was printed on waterproof paper.

Some of his finest illustrations are those done for Paul Gallico's story *The Snow Goose*, which tells how a hunch-backed painter of birds who lived in an East Coast lighthouse was one day brought a wounded Snow Goose by a village girl and tamed it. The painter took his small boat to the beaches at Dunkirk and the goose flew with him, in due course returning alone to bring the news to the

Peter feeding Snow Geese, Slimbridge. The Curator's office/old membership office can be seen in the background

heroine Fritha. The non-illustrated edition came out in 1945 and was clearly inspired by the story Peter had told Gallico about his lighthouse and the Pink-footed Goose, Anabel. Fact and fiction were not directly similar. However, Peter subsequently illustrated the next edition with paintings and line drawings. Much later he supplied the tame Snow Goose and did the drawings for a film of the story made by the BBC.

One of the reasons Peter paints is to educate others, to pass on his enthusiasm for nature in a pleasurable form. In the last forty years pressures of work have allowed him less time for his art and he has held correspondingly fewer exhibitions at Ackermann's, but he has continued to draw and paint every day, finding it both creative and recreational. In the 1950s a change of approach became apparent, which he has described:

> Gradually . . . the likenesses of the birds in my pictures improved, and my earlier works, when I saw them again, left me dissatisfied. Why did I not see when I was painting it that the shape of that wing was all wrong? It stands out a mile now; but I suppose I just did not know enough then. . . . And so the anatomy got better, the lighting became more true and the creatures came to life.

The extent of Peter's perfectionism is demonstrated by the fact that whenever early paintings of his are returned to him for repair work or information he generally corrects any mistakes in the birds and refines the composition. It is not so easy, however, to correct mistakes in watercolour paintings and so he prefers to use oil paints or gouache, an opaque form of watercolour. The many gouaches he has done in his diaries and as pictures in their own right are characterised by an unerring eye for detail and an extremely lifelike portrayal of the animal in question. Most of his larger paintings, however, are in oils. In everything he has done, the whole sum of his experience and knowledge is brought to bear whatever the subject – coral reef fish, whale, insect, reptile, quadruped, bird or Loch Ness Monster – and irrespective of whatever the medium is, oil, gouache, pencil or ballpoint pen.

Another aspect of Peter's determination and

Peter with Tommy Johnston, the rearing pens at Slimbridge

This is Your Life – Uffa Fox,
Eamonn Andrews. Peter was
one of the guests. 1963

perfectionism can be seen in his gliding, which first
began to draw his attention when Bristol Gliding
Club formed its new base at nearby Nympsfield. It
was to become an absorbing and exciting pastime.
His first flight took place in January 1956, and in
June of that year he bought the first in a series of
gliders. The following year he attained the Silver C
gliding badge. He completed his Gold C gliding
badge, achieved the Diamond in 1962, and in 1963
he won the British Gliding Championship.

Catalogue

61. Two Mallard chasing a duck

1954

Oil painting 30 × 25 (76.2 × 63.5)
Private collection

Pictures which are popular with the wildfowling fraternity tend to feature birds which are not too big and not too small, are flying across a landscape of sky, water and marsh, and are of a quarry species of wildfowl. In the 1930s and 1940s many of the artist's pictures followed this pattern, but thereafter it was often abandoned in favour of smaller groups of birds which were given more prominence and painted in greater detail. This painting is a good example of the change of approach.

62. Eyton's Whistling Duck or Plumed Whistling Duck (Australia)

c. 1957

White scraperboard and ink 4 × 6½ (10.1 × 16.4)
Private collection

In November 1956 Peter came across and filmed 130 Plumed Whistling Ducks on a lagoon in the Northern Territory of Australia. This scraperboard drawing was probably done on his return to England.

63. Mallards in a pearly sky

1957

Oil painting 20 × 24 (50 × 60)
Private collection

The pointillist technique used in this picture recalls the dots of pure colour employed by Signac and Seurat in the 1880s and 1890s.

64. Whooper Swans flying low

1958

Oil painting 20 × 30 (50.5 × 76.2)
Tyson Jackson

65. Venice

c. 1961

Ballpoint pen 3¾ × 5½ (9.5 × 14)
The Rt. Hon. Peter Walker MBE MP

This drawing was produced for illustration in the artist's autobiography, *The Eye of the Wind*.

PETER SCOTT
Broadcasting

by *DESMOND HAWKINS*

My first encounter with Peter was dramatic enough to be worth retelling. At the end of the Second World War I joined the BBC in Bristol for the resumption of regional broadcasting, and in 1946 I launched a radio series, *The Naturalist*, which was in effect the flagship of what later became the BBC Natural History Unit. In those early days one of my principal contributors was Ludwig Koch, the pioneer of wildlife sound recording in Britain. Koch's recordings of bird-songs and calls brought an exciting new dimension to radio that I was eager to develop. I commissioned him to record the wintering flocks of White-fronted Geese on the saltings at Slimbridge – a romantically bleak landscape in which the only feature was a gamekeeper's cottage. While we were there Koch said, 'I will let you into a secret. In London there is a rumour that Peter Scott is buying that cottage in order to study the geese.' Who then could have had the vision – except Peter himself – to foresee the transformation of the New

Peter Scott with Desmond
Hawkins, recording *The
Naturalist* (*Photograph Desmond
Hawkins*)

Grounds into the Wildfowl and Wetlands Trust of
today?

When I next drove along the single track to where
the geese were gathered, my way was blocked by an
empty vehicle. Its driver was lying across the
bonnet, holding a telescope. I needed only a quick
glance to say, 'You must be Peter Scott.' 'Yes,' he
replied, 'and you're just in time to see only the sixth
(or was it the eighth?) *Lesser* White-fronted ever
reported in Britain.' He pointed the bird out to me,
among a flock of Common White-front, and passed
me the telescope so that I could see the definitive
gold ring around the bird's eye.

This chance meeting was clearly destined to be
the start of a special relationship! Peter's presence
within little more than 30 miles of Bristol was an
important asset when a new radio series, *Birds in
Britain*, was added to *The Naturalist*. Together with
his friend, James Fisher, Peter became one of the
most popular broadcasters on the radio programmes I produced.

The 1950s brought new opportunities. At that
time Peter was touring the country to drum up
support for his Wildfowl Trust, hiring halls in the
major cities and putting on his own one-man show
during which he talked, drew rapid sketches of
birds and showed film-clips. I meanwhile had gone
to Lime Grove to learn the production techniques
of television, which was about to expand beyond
the London area and reach a national audience.
When I returned to Bristol, Peter told me he
thought his solo fundraising performances would
adapt successfully to television. He invited me to
sit in the audience for one of them and consider
what might be done with it.

At that time all television programmes were
centrally planned and we had no television studio
in Bristol. Fortunately the 'boss' in London was
Cecil McGivern, a war-time colleague of mine
who gave a friendly hearing to our ideas and
decided to let us have a go with two or three
experimental programmes from a studio in Lime
Grove. Undoubtedly Peter's role was crucial. He
was an undisputed authority in his own field, a
gifted draughtsman and an exponent who could
meet a mass audience on popular terms without

condescension. Added to these qualities, his personal charm was decisive. The long-running *Look*
series, with Peter as its host, became one of the
established features of British television in the
fifties and sixties. Among that generation of
viewers he enjoyed a widespread fame which has
probably been rivalled since only by David
Attenborough.

Those first studio programmes soon broadened
their range, with live pictures direct from Slimbridge and the first filming expeditions overseas.
The increasing availability of film reduced the need
for Peter's instant drawings and he developed a
flair for impromptu commentary on film. To
celebrate the Darwin centenary Peter went to the
Galapagos Islands, with Tony Soper as his camera-
man, to make a special programme for *Look*. So
unusual was this that I had to persuade the Peru-
vian ambassador to lend us one of his navy's
vessels as the only means of transport. A dozen
years later I had neighbours departing on package
tours to the Galapagos. In that simple contrast lies
the measure of Peter's achievement in the media.

Much of today's public concern with environmental problems and the need for intelligent and
sensitive conservation has arisen from a ground-
swell of that diffused national opinion to which
politicians are properly alert. I must not over-
estimate the part played by radio and television in
fostering our changing attitudes to wildlife and the
whole ecosystem, for there were other allied forces
at work; but if any one man exemplified the
media's power to generate a fresh imaginative

interest in the natural world it was Peter Scott. And he did it, in a disarmingly easy-looking manner, on everybody's telly.

PETER SCOTT
Gliding

by MICHAEL GARSIDE

When the Bristol Gliding Club moved from Lulsgate to Nympsfield on the Cotswold Edge behind Peter's house at Slimbridge, gliding promised to provide the thrill and the excitement and the occasional fright of competitive yachting which, after Peter's move to Gloucestershire, was not now really within easy reach. It was only a question of time before his competitive spirit would hanker after and finally embrace the British Gliding Championship.

The first glider was a jointly-owned single seat Olympia 2, and its successor a beautiful new sleek Slingsby 'Eagle' with two seats in tandem. The plan was that Peter's family and friends should join in the fun and the enjoyment, but one by one they found that they disliked gliding and were mostly airsick.

At last came my turn, and I was duly strapped into the seat. 'Take up slack.' 'All out.' The tow rope taughtened as the aerotow took us smoothly to 2,200ft in a curious attitude rather higher than the tail of the Tiger Moth which was towing us.

Peter with his Olympia 419, 1960

Suddenly strong 'lift' was indicated – perhaps by instruments, perhaps by one wing tip, perhaps by the seat of the pants, it was all so new to me. In any event, the tow rope released with a click and we were on our own. Engine noise fell away and all was quiet save the whisper of wind in the cockpit canopy and the wings. We were in a thermal, whose heated rising air was stoking a large and ominously black cloud into which we were being sucked. It was rather like driving in dense fog but with a third dimension, and I wondered about other gliders (although there were few about that day) or worse, powered aircraft as they flew through cloud on occasion. But these worries were replaced by the sensation of thermalling.

From the ground gliders in thermals seem to describe large lazy graceful circles, but in practice you sit inclined at anything up to 45 degrees and seem to pivot around an axis, pre-occupied in my case by trying not to be ill. Suddenly all this was irrelevant. We shot out of the murk into bright, bright sun shining from a sky of intense blue and basked in its blissful warmth. Even the whisper of wind died away as we flew straight and level. Between two towers of cloud with tight cauliflower tops the Severn Estuary was etched in astonishing clarity, and we could only look in awe at the wonder and the beauty of it all. Many months later an exhibition of Peter's paintings opened at Ackermann's Gallery in Bond Street, London and one of them reproduced the skyscape of that memorable day.

After that first flight I was often Peter's crew, and would follow to retrieve him with a car and trailer. The FAI (Federation Aeronautique Internationale) had a series of qualifying certificates to encourage aspiring glider pilots. In early 1960 Peter had taken delivery of a new top-of-technology single-seat Olympia 419 sailplane and sought the first available chance to try for the second of three Diamonds for his FAI Gold Badge – a much-coveted and rare prize in Britain. The diamond for a goal flight had already been secured.

A fine day in March with a southerly unstable airstream presented possible conditions, but the radio in the car intimated that Peter was finding it hard work to remain aloft, until Newcastle where a thunder cloud furnished lift, much of it at 1,500ft per minute, to a Diamond *height* of 18,300ft! But its predecessors had flattened out over that part of Britain. At this height the 'glide-out' should have assured the declared destination of Portmoak, north of Edinburgh, but the ground was invisible, and additionally there was no way of knowing the wind speed and direction there. Then a sudden break in the cloud cover pin-pointed Budle Bay and dictated a course which would ensure a landing rather than a splash-down in the North Sea. The Scottish border was crossed at 4,000ft, and with no hope of reaching Portmoak without further 'lift' – a rare thing in the evening. Just before 7.00 p.m. Cockburnspath provided a field – 14 miles short of the Diamond distance of 312 miles. But no one flew further in Britain that year, the flight qualified for the Wakefield Trophy, and the pilot had been away from home for only 23 hours.

Congratulations Peter on your eighty years in which you have taken every opportunity to enjoy and understand the natural wonders of the world around you, and made it possible for thousands more of us to do the same.

6 TRAVEL AND WORLD CONSERVATION

In the late 1950s concern was growing that human progress would precipitate an ecological tragedy. The toxic chemicals which were indiscriminately being used in the countryside to exterminate pests were entering the food chain and causing mortality and infertility in many birds and mammals, as was signally pointed out in Rachel Carson's book *Silent Spring*. Peter began to think more ecologically and environmentally and took positive steps to ensure the survival of endangered species. From 1953 he was involved in the International Union for Conservation of Nature and Natural Resources (IUCN), whose Survival Service Commission was set up to prevent 'the extinction of species, subspecies and discrete populations thereby maintaining genetic diversity'. Peter became its Chairman and initiated the Red Data Books which list endangered species. Listing was, however, only the first step in an uphill struggle to find out why they are threatened and persuade the relevant authorities to take the necessary action.

At this time the conservation movement was

With a Koala in Australia

badly in need of funds. It could not rely on government support and so, in 1961, it was decided at an IUCN meeting in Switzerland that a separate fund-raising organisation should be set up. Along with Max Nicholson and Julian Huxley, Peter was one of the founders of the new charity, which was to be called the World Wildlife Fund (now the World Wide Fund for Nature). He designed the Fund's famous panda logo, planned its structure and became Chairman not only of WWF International but also the British National Appeal. He saw the Fund as a new Noah's Ark which would safeguard the present diversity of wildlife in reserves and national parks, until such time as man would overcome the problem of overpopulation and want to live in harmony with nature once again. These and other ideas were summed up in a conservation creed he wrote at the time:

> What man did to the Dodo, and has since been doing to the Blue Whale and about 1,000 other kinds of animals, may or may not be morally wrong. But the conservation of nature is most important because of what nature does for man.
>
> I believe something goes wrong with man when he cuts himself off from the natural world. I think he knows it, and this is why he keeps gardens and window-boxes and house plants, and dogs and cats and budgerigars. Man does not live by bread alone. I believe he should take just as great pains to look after the natural treasures which inspire him as he does to pre-

Right
Peter at the International Whaling Commission meeting, Brighton, 1982
(Photograph Elizabeth Kemf/ WWF)

79.   Self-portrait with wife and Humpback Whales, 1979 (p. 120)

85.   Procreation, Oleander Hawk Moths, 1981 (p. 124)

serve his man-made treasures in art galleries and museums. This is a responsibility we have to future generations.

Over the years Peter has been a tireless campaigner for the World Wildlife Fund and conservation. Chairing meetings, attending conferences, liaising with heads of state, lecturing, fund-raising and visiting habitats and reserves has taken him all over the world, always in a voluntary capacity. Achieving results takes a great deal of time and effort, as is exemplified by the anti-whaling campaign with which he has been involved for over twenty years. From 1965 he was conservation adviser to the British delegation of the International Whaling Commission, the body which was finally able twenty years later to enforce a moratorium on all commercial whaling. Prior to this Peter deepened his own understanding of the whales and their plight by entering the world they inhabit and swimming underwater with them, while on another occasion he witnessed the harpooning and slow death of a Minke whale. He has given press conferences on the issue and recently returned the Icelandic Order of the Falcon (awarded to him in 1971) because of Iceland's stance on whaling.

By 1980 the World Wildlife Fund had set up National Appeals in twenty-six countries. WWF Australia was launched, with Peter's help, in 1979, and later that year he went to China to establish a firm conservation link and get a programme going for the giant panda. This was the first time an international conservation body had been invited

Right
WWF's own panda symbol meets its live counterpart in Beijing Zoo, as Peter looks on (*Photograph Nancy Nash/ WWF*)

into the People's Republic, with the result that a WWF China Committee was set up and an agreement signed to confirm the country's full cooperation in conservation. A year later Peter was in Peking to launch the World Conservation Strategy, a document which stresses that if human development is to be sustained it must be linked to the conservation of living resources, setting out guidelines on how this can be achieved. The panda project was also advanced by a visit to Sichuan province to select a suitable place for a research centre, towards which the World Wildlife Fund gave one million dollars. Peter believes the many visits and friendly discussions brought a new attitude to conservation in China and encouraged protective measures in the case of pandas, whales and other endangered species.

Peter's knowledge of wildlife and their habitats the world over is founded on the first-hand experience he has acquired by extensive travelling. Over the years, he has visited most of the countries of the world in connection with his work for television and conservation and also as a naturalist on board the *Linblad Explorer*, a 2,500 ton mini-liner which specialised in taking passengers to remote corners of the earth. Frequently he travelled abroad six or more times a year, usually with a hectic itinerary when he reached his destination including guided tours, reception committees, television interviews and lectures. In June 1969 his travel schedule was more hectic than usual. At the beginning of the month there was a trip to Rejkjavik in a successful bid to prevent the flooding of the breeding ground of the Pink-footed geese. He then travelled to Italy to attend a WWF board meeting and receive an audience at the Vatican with Pope Paul XI. Finally, at the end of the month, he journeyed to Alaska to advise BP on a safe route for a new oil pipeline, taking account of the environment and its wildlife.

In 1956 Peter and his wife, Philippa visited the Great Barrier Reef in Australia and had their first introduction to underwater fish-watching, an experience he wrote about in his diary:

> For a part of these 3 days I have been in a new world. Nothing I have done in natural history in all my life has stirred me quite so sharply. . . . The dramatic threshold which is crossed as soon as one first puts one's face mask below the surface is, to a naturalist nothing less than staggering in its impact. Much has been written about the scarcely explored new continent of the ocean . . . and yet I was unprepared for the visionary revelation when I first saw the real thing.

Since then Peter and Philippa have dived and snorkelled to study fish in the Indian Ocean, the Red Sea, the Arctic, the Antarctic, the Caribbean and the South, West and Central Pacific. Their specialities are Butterfly, Angel, Cherub and Clown fish, but they have also swum underwater with sea lions, seals, penguins, dugongs, manatees, dolphins and whales. The great diversity of marine life has given Peter cause to ponder on the

Peter scuba diving – fish-watching

evolution of behaviour patterns as much as patterns of colour and shape, enabling him to draw parallels with the world of birds.

The last two decades have seen a great expansion of the Wildfowl Trust since its establishment at Slimbridge in 1946. It made a direct contribution to the conservation of wildfowl and wetlands through its refuges and its widespread membership. The first branch opened at Peakirk near Peterborough in 1957 and was followed by further centres at Welney in Cambridgeshire, Caerlaverock near Dumfries, Martin Mere in Lancashire, Washington in County Durham and Arundel in Sussex. At the same time the Slimbridge site expanded with, amongst other things, the building of a research, visitor and education centre. Some of the branches are purely reserves while others combine this facility with a tame wildfowl collection. Peter has been closely involved in the development programme which has allowed him to create what he has termed 'wildfowl landscapes on the ground', with their combination of ponds, screen-banks, hides, walkways and observation towers.

The visible success of the Trust is evident in its visitor figures of over three quarters of a million people a year, and something like 10½ million visitors since 1946. But there is also the 'invisible' success of work carried on behind the scenes. This has included the breeding of endangered species in captivity. There was the rescue of the Hawaiian Goose – down to less than 50 birds in 1950. From 3 birds, with a subsequent addition of 4 more for fresh blood, the Trust was able to send 50 young birds to Hawaii each year for four years. Currently the Trust raises some 60–70 Ne-Ne goslings each year and has distributed the species to most of the world's zoos. Repopulation programmes are currently in progress for the Whiteheaded Duck in Hungary and the White-winged Wood Duck in India and South-east Asia. The invention of portable incubators means that hatching eggs can be moved long distances, even from continent to continent, and adult birds need hardly ever be taken from the wild. The Wildfowl Trust has come a long way from the time when its headquarters were three cottages at the end of a lane, and Peter wondered how it would catch up with research stations in Canada and America!

Peter, *c.* 1961

Peter has received many awards in recognition of his distinguished work as a conservationist, naturalist and painter. In 1952 he was awarded the CBE as Honorary Director and founder of the Wildfowl Trust, and in 1973 he was the first person ever to be knighted for services to conservation. He has been Rector of Aberdeen University and Chancellor of the University of Birmingham. In the last decade an American museum elected him Wildlife Artist of the Year, while a scientist named a new fish after him, *Cirrhilabrus scottorum* (the plural is to include his wife who was also diving at the time it was found). In 1987 he was made a Companion of Honour and elected a Fellow of the Royal Society, and currently he is, amongst other things, President of the Fauna and Flora Preservation Society, President of the British Butterfly Conservation Society and Honorary Chairman of the Council of the World Wide Fund for Nature (International).

The prospect of being eighty years old is not inducing Peter to take life at a more leisurely pace. In the last year he has done interviews for radio and television, travelled a good deal and had a retrospective flight in a glider over Slimbridge. An exhibition of his most recent paintings was held at Ackermann's in March and sold out after only a few days. There has been the usual steady stream of commissions for new pictures, a visit to Washington to collect yet another conservation award, and the Wildfowl Trust's change of name. In September 1989 the Trust will open an eighth centre at Strangford Lough in Northern Ireland,

Peter in his father's hut at
Cape Evans, Antarctica, 1971

and in 1990 another at Llanelli in Wales. The Trust will then have centres in all parts of the United Kingdom. In addition, there is the exciting possibility of a London presence at Barn Elms Reservoir close to Hammersmith Bridge.

Peter has a dream for Slimbridge. This involves a major building programme as the Trust expands its education, research and conservation activities. Nothing would make him happier than for all his eightieth birthday presents to go towards making his dream a reality.

His concept of World Park status for the Antarctic Continent, which he has been promoting for many years, suddenly appears to have become a practical possibility with powerful backing from the Australian Government.

When it comes to a personal ambition still to be fulfilled – asked recently, Peter replied 'To paint a *really* good picture'.

Catalogue

66.   The Natural World of Man

1963

Oil painting 28 × 36 (71.1 × 90.2)
Private collection

This picture represents man's dilemma in his
relationship with nature. The problem is seen as
triangular. At the pointed end are ethical
responsibilities to save the animals facing
extinction – the Blue Whale, the Whooping
Crane, Hispaniolan Solenodon, Tuatara,
Galapagos Tortoise, Rhinoceros. From there the
scope broadens to encompass communities of
animals – wild geese, fishes, antelopes – and their
relationship to flowers and trees and to water and
soil. All are a part of the biosphere in which man
must live. The water is in the cumulus cloud
(under which a white glider soars), and the river
system with its tree-like formation, bearing
leaves, and its foam-polluted tributary, is echoed
by the pattern of soil erosion caused by the over-
grazing of cattle being herded below with their
accompanying dust. There are suggestions of
urbanization and industrialization. A ship gives
out oil pollution, a plane is spraying toxic
chemicals, and there is a rocket missile. The peak
of Everest ('because it is there') peeps from
behind the mushroom cloud whose fall-out is
destroying the people spreading from the
population explosion. 'The pill' is there too.

The three-dimensional triangle itself is carried by arms in a sea of space dominated by the moon, with a nearby sputnik. In the right-hand corner a new galaxy is born.

Man, with one white and one black hand, stands transfixed before this vast and terrifying pyramid of problems.

(Colour plate)

67. Bewick's Swans against the setting November sun

1968

Oil painting 20 × 30 (51.6 × 77.1)
Private collection

Four years before this picture was painted Peter began an intensive study of the Bewick's Swans which winter on the Severn estuary. He and his daughter Dafila noticed that each swan had its own unique bill pattern and could therefore be identified wherever it was seen. They studied the swans' social and family behaviour, visited the breeding grounds in Arctic Rusia and put out food for them on the pond in front of the studio window, so that between 300 and 400 are now attracted there each winter. Some have been coming now for twenty-five consecutive winters.

Painting swans against the light presents a special challenge. Some of it shines through their wings, some is reflected off the water, and some down from the sky.

68.   Pintails on a hazy day

1969

Oil painting 20 × 30 (50.5 × 76)
Private collection

The setting for this picture is the great marsh of the Coto Doñana in the delta of the River Guadalquivir in southern Spain, where large numbers of our northern ducks go in the winter. The Pintail has always been one of Peter's favourite ducks and he particularly enjoys painting it for its elegance and distinctive plumage. As a species the bird is circumpolar and probably ranks as the second most numerous duck after the Mallard.

69. Red-breasted Geese in the big field below the quarry at Sinoie

1970

Oil painting 18 × 14 (45.5 × 35.6)
Private collection

This picture is a bird's eye view of a large flock of Red-breasted Geese. The artist first saw these birds in large numbers in November 1969 in Romania, and the trip led to further visits in the winters of 1971, 1973 and 1977. In 1971 his objectives were to count the geese as part of a long-term population study, learn more about their winter habits, photograph them, and by taking an interest in them encourage the Romanians to do the same.

70. Canada Geese and Canvas Backs in Maryland

1971

Oil painting 20 × 24 (50.8 × 61)
Private collection

71. Portrait of Jenny Agutter

1971

Pencil 12 × 9¾ (30.5 × 24.7)
Private collection

The sitter played the part of Fritha in the BBC film of Paul Gallico's story *The Snow Goose* (see p. 86 for Peter's involvement with the book and the film).

115

72. Comings and goings at high water – Dunlins, Curlew Sandpiper and Brents

1973

Oil painting 20 × 30 (50.8 × 76.2)
R.D. Franklin

Ducks, geese and swans are only a part of the ecology of our wetlands. The habitats sustain many other species, including wading birds such as Dunlins, and this is why it is so important to preserve them.

73. Bewick's Swans over Welney

1973

Gouache 8 × 5¾ (20.3 × 14.6)
R.D. Franklin

The Wildfowl and Wetlands Trust Refuge in the
Ouse Washes near Welney consists of 850 acres
of pure wetland habitat. Here up to 2,000
Bewick's Swans, 30,000 Wigeon and thousands
of other ducks can be seen from the observatory.

74. Coral reef fishes

1973

Oil painting 24 × 36 (61 × 91.4)
Private collection

Over the last thirty-three years coral reefs have
provided Peter with some of his most
memorable experiences as a naturalist. The
amazing visibility, the beautiful colours and
shapes and the sheer diversity of species have
made him into a compulsive skin-diver and fish-
watcher. On some days he has identified up to
180 different species in a couple of hours, listing
them on his white plastic underwater drawing
board with accompanying illustrations drawn
from life.

(Colour plate)

75. Barnacle Geese with Criffel beyond

1974

Oil on canvas 20 × 24 (50.8 × 61)
Private collection

When Peter first visited the Solway Firth in December 1928 several thousand Barnacle Geese could be seen. The numbers declined, however, and by the 1940s only 400 birds wintered there. The site has been a Wildfowl Trust Refuge since 1971 and with increased protection the population has grown to over 12,000. In 1974 four leucistic birds (white, but without the pink eyes of a true albino) were in the flock and were later caught and ringed at their breeding ground in Spitzbergen. Two of them can be seen in this picture.

76. Wigeon in the afternoon – Chew Valley Lake

1975

Oil painting 28 × 36 (71.1 × 91.4)
Mr and Mrs A.L. Richards

The location for this painting is a large reservoir south of Bristol which provides facilities for sailing, fishing and birdwatching, each within carefully defined areas. In catering for a variety of recreational needs the water authority has, in the artist's opinion, shown some skill and imagination.

77. Courtship in Loch Ness – Loch Ness Monsters

1975

Oil painting 16 × 19 (40.6 × 48.2)
Mrs Jaquette James, Torosay Castle, Isle of Mull,
where the picture is on display in the summer
months

The artist believes there is a consistency in the
reports of the animals which so many people
claim to have seen down the years in the loch.
There is a hard core of observations, films, sonar
traces and photographs which are difficult to
explain in terms of known phenomena or
described animals. In 1975 Peter and Robert
Rines published an article in *Nature* in which
they gave 'Nessie' a scientific name, *Nessiteras
rhombopteryx*, (the Ness monster with diamond-
shaped fin), thus enabling it to be protected once
its existence can be established beyond doubt. He
has dived in the loch twice but never seen one of
the animals, and although he keeps an open mind
as to its existence, he finds it rather harder to
believe that the animal is there after so long a
time without convincingly showing itself.
Taking all the descriptions and photographs into
account, the picture gives his impression of what
the animals might look like if they are there.

(Colour plate)

78. Barnacle Geese, with Criffel beyond

1976

Ink and wash 5½ × 8½ (14 × 21.6)
R.D. Franklin

79. Self-portrait with wife and Humpback Whales

1979

Oil painting 24 × 36 (61 × 91.4)
Private collection

In March 1979 Peter and his wife had an unforgettable experience when they swam with Humpback Whales off the Hawaian island of Maui. In the course of one 21 minute period of snorkelling seven whales came to look at them. Peter is swimming at the surface in the centre, while at the left Philippa is taking photographs. Although Humpback Whales grow to over 40ft long and can weigh up to 45 tons, throughout the meeting the whales were absolutely gentle and gave no cause to be afraid.

(Colour plate)

80. The first Pinkfeet touched down on the flooded field this side of the sycamores

1980

Oil painting 15 × 18 (38.1 × 45.4)
Lent by kind permission of HRH Prince Philip, The Duke of Edinburgh

The stippling effect in this picture was produced
by taking a pair of discarded tights, rolling them
into a ball and dabbing it onto paint which was
initially applied to the canvas using a palette
knife.

81.   In the morning the Pinkfeet flew down the creek to drink and wash

1980

Oil painting 10 × 14 (25.4 × 35.5)
Lent by kind permission of HRH The Prince of Wales

82.   A raft of Scaup

1981

Oil painting 14 × 10 (35.5 × 25.4)
Lent by kind permission of HRH The Prince of Wales

The Scaup, a marine species of diving duck, occurs on several parts of our coasts and estuaries in winter. Its gregarious habits provided the idea for this small picture which makes the most of the patterning of plumage and posture present in the scene. All the ducks except two are asleep and have their bills tucked under their wings.

83.   Upland Geese in the Falkland Islands

1981

Oil painting 20 × 24 (50.8 × 61)
Private collection

There are two sub-species of Upland Geese, otherwise known as Magellan Geese. Lesser Magellan Geese, as shown here, are residents of the Falkland Islands. They are still common despite ruthless persecution due to their habit of

feeding on grass, which is needed for sheep. The male of the species is predominantly white, while the female is deep reddish cinnamon. The artist has paid several visits to the Falkland Islands. He was instrumental in forming the Falkland Islands Foundation to encourage research and conservation and to monitor the environmental well-being of the Archipelago.

84. Pink-eared Ducks

1981

Gouache 10 × 7 (25.4 × 17.8)
Mr and Mrs C.H. Taylour

The artist saw Pink-eared Ducks for the first
time in the bush near Perth, Australia in 1956.
They came across the birds on a stagnant river
which in many places was spanned from bank to
bank by dead bushes and trees. Although they
managed to film the ducks they could not get
quite close enough to see their pink ears – the
characteristics of plumage which were visible
were the black head marking, the striped flanks,
the white forehead and warm buff on the under
tail covers. The broad flat beak with little
curtains near the tip is also very distinctive.

85. Procreation, Oleander Hawk Moths

1981

Oil painting 36 × 28 (91.4 × 71.2)
Private collection

Since his school days Peter has had a great
interest in hawk-moths. One of the rarest and
most beautiful in Britain is the Oleander Hawk
Moth, which only occasionally reaches this
country from its strongholds in Asia and Africa.
The first live specimens which Peter saw were
caterpillars that he found in 1969 during a visit to
Qatar to look at a captive herd of Arabian Oryx.
He took them home to Slimbridge and bred

three generations of them, feeding them on periwinkle.

(Colour plate)

86. Peter and Philippa with some of their favourite animals

1982

Oil painting 36 × 28 (91.4 × 71.1)
Private collection

This picture is an attempt to bring together on one canvas some of the favourite animals of the artist and his wife. If anything, scale is inverted so that the Oleander Hawk Moth is the largest image and the Humpback Whale at the top is the smallest. But there are no rules in art, least of all to say how big an animal should be painted. The animals depicted are, from top left: Batfish, Humpback Whale, Hawaiian Goose, Impala, Greenland Whitefront, Oleander Hawk Moth, Red-breasted Goose, Ruddy Duck, White-fronted Geese, Giant Panda, Lesser White-fronted Goose, Teal, Bewick's Swans, Puss Moth larva, Pintail, Peter and Phil, Butterfly Fish, Praying Mantis, 'Spookie' (Blue Merle Collie), Chamaeleon, Green Tree Frog.

(Colour plate)

87. Pinkfeet coming in from the Solway, across the Blackshaw Bank

1983

Oil painting 20 × 30 (50.8 × 76.2)
Private collection

88. Wigeon over a grey sea

1985

Oil painting 15 × 18 (38.1 × 45.7)
Private collection

89. The Mermaid and the Blue Planet

1985

Oil painting 24 × 20 (61 × 50.8)
Mr and Mrs Laurin H. Healy

This allegorical picture stresses the fragility of life on earth. A mermaid holds the planet protectively while hands try to grasp it from her, the snake-like pattern on the wing tips of a moth whispering temptation in her ear. Arranged around the figure are some of the Scotts' favourite animals – Cuttle Fish, Chamaeleon, Dolphin, Sea Horse, Barnacle Goose and the White Whale. Because this species of whale is believed to be the most intelligent marine mammal the formula $E = MC^2$ may well be held in its brain. Why should it not carry Einstein's equation in its memory?

90. The Snow Goose

1987

Gouache 7½ × 10½ (19 × 26.7)
R.D. Franklin

This is the Snow Goose of the Paul Gallico story
(see p. 86).

91. Dafila Scott: Portrait of Sir Peter Scott

1989

Oil painting 18 × 14 (45.7 × 35.6)
Private collection

The artist portrayed by his daughter.

(Colour plate)

92. Puffins

1989

Gouache 7⅛ × 5⅛ (17.8 × 12.8)
Private collection

(Colour plate)

PETER SCOTT

Conservationist

by MAX NICHOLSON

During at least the past two centuries, since the
appearance of Gilbert White's *Natural History of
Selborne*, the pursuit of natural history has enlisted
the affection and enthusiasm of a growing number
of perceptive people, perhaps especially in England
and Scotland, and in the Netherlands. Recently it
has blossomed out into a key science, Ecology,
with a strong cross-disciplinary influence, perhaps
less upon other sciences than upon public opinion
and those willingly or unwillingly involved in
applying it in conservation, physical planning and
economic development. Some of these have
sought to dismiss it as 'the environmental lobby',
fervently hoping and wishfully expecting it to
prove a transient fashion which would soon go
away. To their dismay, by 1989 it has been proved
to even the dimmest and most reactionary that far
from going away it has come to stay, on a scale and
with consequences much more far-reaching than
their worst previous fears.

This revolution, enforced by the collapse of

mankind's brief excesses as the supposed master of Nature, and given its positive content by natural history, ecology and conservation, has achieved its current success through the leadership and team-work of a small but remarkable group, among whom none has made a more decisive contribution than Peter Scott. Born a naturalist and a traveller (although he was not allowed at his then tender age to accept my invitation to accompany us to Greenland in 1928) he early developed his skill at painting to such a point as to free him from the need to become tied to any paid job. By becoming a leader in the special realm of waterfowl painting he enabled himself to combine freedom with getting into the centre of a fast growing branch of natural history, and of a new world of film and television communication.

By now we are so accustomed to his role as a conservationist that we may easily forget how long it took to graft his outstanding gifts as a presenter on television and other media onto the practical and specific conservation mission which he had embarked upon with the foundation of the Severn Wildfowl Trust in November 1946. (As a then member of the Council I was relieved to find that at our first Annual General Meeting we had only overspent our income by slightly more than 100 per cent, calling to our aid the Stock of Birds which was helpfully valued at slightly more to balance the Accounts.)

I cannot forbear to quote from the Trust's first Annual Report the two-line note, 'Miss Philippa Talbot-Ponsonby is now Assistant Secretary and

Philippa Talbot-Ponsonby with Greylag Geese, Slimbridge, 1949

has picked up the rather complicated threads of the Trust's activities with great efficiency.' No appreciation of Peter Scott can fail to echo very loudly this modest tribute to the services of Lady Scott, not only to the Trust but to the conservation of Peter himself.

As early as 1950 the opportunity was taken to come to the rescue of the Hawaiian Goose, then reduced to no more than forty survivors, about half of which were in captivity. This bold and eventually triumphantly successful project was thought at the time almost to call for apology, for it 'although a new departure, falls without doubt within the objects for which the Trust was formed. A practical contribution to the preservation of a vanishing species is a matter of worldwide significance.'

It was, however, only during its second decade, some time after the Wildfowl Trust had dropped its cosy but localised 'Severn' prefix, that the tasks of conservation and research at home and abroad became dominant, the turning-point being the jestingly titled 'BBC/IUCN Darwin Centenary Expedition to the British Virgin Islands, Trinidad, Panama, Ecuador and the Galapagos Islands' of January–March 1959. This was a landmark in Peter's involvement in international Conservation, especially since it coincided with the establishment, by agreement with the government of Ecuador, of the Charles Darwin Research Station, the prototype for a series of field stations with international status. At the same time it promoted the involvement of the BBC in world wildlife and environmental filming, which has since proved such a decisive influence in building up the popular movement.

Shortly after this, Peter became interested in raising a large world fund by eliciting donations from a number of targeted millionaires. However, this proved difficult, and in 1961 he agreed to come in with me on an alternative project, which quickly took shape between April and September 1961 as the World Wildlife Fund (recently renamed the World Wide Fund for Nature). The full story of this is related in WWF's first report, *The Launching of a New Ark* (1965), and in *Saving the Animals* (1981), written for WWF by Bernard Stonehouse, with an introduction by Peter in which he traces back his own involvement in conservation to 1935.

I recently had occasion in *The New Environmental Age* (1987) to compare and contrast the personalities and contributions to the conservation movement of a number of its founders whom I had had the privilege of knowing and working with in action. Of some two dozen singled out for this treatment, all except two were no longer with us, and one of these two was Peter, whom it would have been absurd to omit, although in the circumstances he was mentioned only in a few lines.

Here is another opportunity to try to place his contribution in perspective. That perspective must, however summarily, take account of the complex and fast-changing nature of the modern conservation challenge; the depth and breadth of the scientific, social, technological and political implications, and the blend of personal qualities,

Peter with a Bronze-wing Duck from South America. Bronze-wings have bred regularly at Slimbridge

talents, experience and capabilities called for in order to tackle them successfully with time fast running out. The rate of world change and of human impact on the environment has not yet ceased accelerating in a way that has called for acute and flexible perception and versatile responses, in both of which Peter has excelled. As when he is painting ducks, he looks and listens intently at those who confront or offer help to him, and he is rarely mistaken about their characters and motives. Again, as in painting, he focusses intensely on the essentials and is thus able to present facts and issues vividly and persuasively. (He once wanted to stand for Parliament but in the interests of conservation I vigorously dissuaded him.)

One of the few among his gifts that he has perhaps not wholly managed to bring to bear effectively in the conservation movement has been his deep ethical concern, which many conservationists react to with slight embarrassment; here perhaps he is a bit before his time. In almost every other respect he is perfectly matched to grapple with the misconceptions and misdeeds of this sorry century. As such a public personification of the perfect model of a modern conservationist it may well be that providing a pattern for many of his baffled and lost contemporaries to try to follow has been not the least of his varied gifts to the cause.

PETER SCOTT
Travels

by NIGEL SITWELL

Peter Scott was one of my earliest heroes. In 1946 I was given *The Battle of the Narrow Seas*, his book about his wartime exploits as a naval officer in the English Channel. Though not written for children, it was just the sort of exciting, stiff-upper-lip, 'Boys'-Own-Paper' stuff to appeal to a schoolboy in those days.

Later, I came to know and admire his paintings, and found a further reason for admiration when I learned about his flying skills, for I too became a pilot, though of powered aircraft not gliders.

It would have been terribly disappointing, when I finally met him – in 1962, soon after the World Wildlife Fund was launched – if I had not liked him, or found that he failed to live up to my expectations. But fortunately he did live up to them. And I discovered that he has a gift for inspiring others, partly by example but also by his logical arguments, his determined commitment to the causes that he champions – and especially by his obvious enthusiasm and enjoyment of all that he is involved in.

On the *Lindblad Explorer* expedition to Campbell Island, 1971. Peter is seated centre. Amongst others in the picture are Roger Tory Peterson and Keith Shackleton

Travelling has long been a major part of Peter's life, which is something else I share with him. And on several occasions our paths have crossed as we circled the globe.

Once, we visited the Seychelles on board the M.S. *Lindblad Explorer*. Peter's wife Philippa and daughter Dafila were also with him on board, and together we explored the Seychelles' wonderful coral reefs. The Scott family at that time had some rather superior face-masks that allowed them to talk to one another as they snorkelled their way through the water. They tended to swim in a

86.   Peter and Philippa with some of their favourite animals, 1982 (p. 125)

92. Puffins, 1989 (p. 127)

V-formation, rather like a skein of geese, while I maintained a position out to one side. Peter led the way, telling us the Latin names of the fish we encountered. Phil and Dafila were able to comment or ask questions, as I recall, but I – having only the standard mask – could not do so. Occasionally I forgot this, however, and opened my mouth to speak, only to get a mouthful of water instead of participation in the ichthyological discourse.

It should be said that such masks are frowned upon nowadays; and the Scotts themselves no longer use them. But the story does emphasize Peter's delight in informing, explaining, and in sharing his tremendous enjoyment of the natural world – even while he is under water.

On the same trip, I and the other passengers were deeply impressed when we joined him in the ship's bar during the cocktail hour, and saw the ease with which he would paint, from memory, the fish he had seen that day.

For one who has travelled so much, and to so many out of the way places, Peter has seldom been in serious danger. But there was major cause for concern quite recently, in May 1989. Ironically, he was not threatened by a close encounter with a shark, or a man-eating tiger, or an aggressive grizzly, but by a humble – though highly toxic – cheeseburger! He and Philippa were on their way to Virgin Gorda, in the West Indies, for a few days fish-watching before going to the United States to raise funds for the Wildfowl and Wetlands Trust, when Peter had the unfortunate burger at a stopover. The food-poisoning was serious enough for Richard Branson to come to the rescue with a helicopter so that Peter could be airlifted to civilisation.

Peter's travels have been undertaken for a variety of reasons, and some of his most notable journeys have been made on behalf of WWF or other conservation organizations. One particularly significant mission was to China, in 1979, to open up direct – and as it turned out, important and continuing – links between that vast nation and the world conservation community. Peter was the ideal ambassador. He had chosen and drawn the giant panda that was WWF's famous symbol. He was a naturalist, author, and many other things besides. The Chinese believe that there is more to life than 'business' (notwithstanding that the business on that occasion was something as comparatively unmaterialistic as nature conservation). They admire most, and get along with best, the well-rounded, cultured person who has a wide range of interests. Furthermore, he was seventy years old, and the Chinese have a well-known respect for age and the sagacity that is presumed to go with advancing years. Peter himself enjoys recounting how the Chinese accorded him particular esteem because, as he said, he was 'an old man'.

There is no doubt that Peter has been the most valuable asset of WWF, the global conservation body that he helped to found in 1961, and also of the Wildfowl and Wetlands Trust, which was his personal vision and which was established in 1946.

To understand why, one must return to his own enjoyment of wildlife and wild places, and his ability to share this with others. These days there is abundant talk of vanishing rainforests, decreasing biodiversity, and lost gene pools. Science and statistics are certainly vitally important foundations of nature conservation, but the fact remains that for most people, and that includes government ministers as well as the rest of us, the strongest appeal is to the emotions.

Peter's unique talent for communication, and his evident love of wild animals and plants, have been immensely persuasive. If he had not been around to steer the modern conservation movement, the scientists would have found it far more difficult getting their message so widely heard and understood.

BIBLIOGRAPHY

Sir Peter Scott's first illustrations were published in a book as long ago as 1924, when he was only fifteen years old. Seven illustrations were accepted by Evelyn Cheesman for her book *Everyday Doings of Insects*.

Since then illustrations have appeared in many books and he is the author of 25. The long running *Wildfowl*, the Wildfowl Trust's annual report bears special mention. This publication first appeared in 1948 as *The Severn Wildfowl Trust Annual Report*; Last year's copy was number 39. In the early days this report related the happenings at Slimbridge, however, as the years passed, it has become a collection of scientific papers. Over the years some 1,000 plus illustrations of Sir Peter's have been included and these are some of his finest pen and ink drawings. The largest collection of drawings is to be found in the seventh Annual report 1953–4, in which there are 100 pen and ink drawings. A colour reproduction has been used on the cover of every report.

The best book, in which to find a complete cross-section of the artists work, *Observations of Wildlife* was published in 1980 by Phaidon, with a recent reprint. It contains a collection of work covering a period of 40 years, and has 39 coloured plates with 66 other illustrations.

The canvas room, Slimbridge, *c.* 1955

The following list has been a labour of love which has been put together over the last ten years. The books are listed as they were published, in London unless otherwise stated.

PAUL WALKDEN, 1989

1. Books Written and Illustrated or Edited

Morning Flight. Country Life. Signed limited edition of 750 copies 1935. Further editions; April 1936, November 1936, November 1937, October 1939, May 1941, August 1942, May 1944, August 1946, September 1947, November 1949 and November 1950.

Wild Chorus. Country Life. Signed limited edition of 1250 copies 1938. Further editions; September 1939, November 1939, April 1941, September 1942, May 1944, April 1946, April 1947, December 1948 and November 1949.

The Battle of the Narrow Seas. Country Life. 1945. Further edition 1946.

Portrait Drawings. Country Life. 1949, all signed.

Key to the Wildfowl of the World. Severn Wildfowl Trust. First appeared in the Second Annual Report 1948–9. 1949. It was reprinted as a separate booklet in 1950 with a revised edition in 1951.

Wild Geese and Eskimos. Country Life. 1951.

Nature Parliament, A Book of Broadcasts. With Newman, L.H. and Fisher, J. (ed.) Dent. 1952.

A Thousand Geese. With Fisher, J. Collins. 1953. Further edition 1954.

The Geography, Birds and Mammals of the Perry River Region. With Hanson, H.C. and Queneau, P. The Arctic Institute of North America. 1956.

Wildfowl of the British Isles. With Boyd, H. Country Life. 1957.

A Coloured Key to the Wildfowl of the World. Wildfowl Trust. 1957. Further editions; 1961, 1965, 1968, 1972, 1977 and 1988.

Faraway Look One. With Scott, P. Cassell. 1960.

Faraway Look Two. With Scott, P. Cassell. 1960.

The Eye of the Wind. Hodder and Stoughton. 1961. Further editions; June 1961, July 1961, 1962, 1963, 1966, 1966, 1967, 1967, 1968 and 1977.

Animals in Africa. With Scott, P. Cassell. 1962.

Waterfowl. Berkshire Printing Co. 1963.

My Favourite Stories of Wildlife. (editor). Illustrated by Shackleton, K. Lutterworth. 1965.

The Launching of a New Ark. (editor). Collins. 1965.

Happy the Man. Sitwell, N. editor. Sphere. 1967.

The Wild Swans at Slimbridge. With Scott, P. Wildfowl Trust. 1970.

The Living World of Animals. (editor). Readers Digest. 1970.

The Swans. With The Wildfowl Trust. Michael Joseph. 1972, 24 copies leather bound and signed.

Conservation in Mauritius. Privately printed. 1973.

Mitchell Beazley World Atlas of Birds. (editor). Mitchell Beazley. 1974. ·

The Amazing World of Animals. (editor). Nelson. 1975.

Observations of Wildlife. Phaidon. Signed limited edition of 200 copies 1980. Further editions; 1981 and 1987.

The Swans Fly In. With Scott, P. Wildfowl Trust. 1983.

Travel Diaries of a Naturalist 1. Collins/Harvill. 1983.

Travel Diaries of a Naturalist 2. Collins/Harvill. 1985.

Travel Diaries of a Naturalist 3. Collins/Harvill. 1987.

2. Books and Booklets Illustrated in Whole, or in Part

Everyday Doings of Insects. Cheesman, E. 7 b/w illustrations. Harrap. 1924. Further edition 1930.

Adventures Among Birds. Schoolboys, Three. Privately printed. 1926. (525 copies only printed).

Waterfowl and Game Birds in Captivity. Moody, A.F. (2 photographs) 1932.

Wildfowl. Player, J. & sons. 25 colour cigarette cards. 1936.

Prospectus. West London Shooting Ground. 13 pencil drawings. 1936.

A Bird in the Bush. Kennet, Lord. Signed limited edition; 550 copies, 3 colour plates & 24 b/w illustrations. Ordinary edition; 1 colour plate & 24 b/w illustrations. Country Life. Both editions 1936.

At the Turn of the Tide. Perry, R. Coloured frontispiece. Drummond. 1938.

Grey Goose. Bratby, M. Colour frontispiece with 25 b/w illustrations. Bles. 1939.

A Book on Duck Shooting. Campen Heilner, V. 3 photographs. New York, Knapf. 1939.

The Handbook of British Birds. Witherby, H.F. 10 colour illustrations. Volume 3. Witherby. 4 volume set, 1938–41.

Through the Air. Bratby, M. 25 b/w illustrations. Country Life. 1941.

The Snow Goose. Gallico, P. 750 copies, Special edition, signed by author and illustrator. 4 colour plates and 24 pen-and-ink drawings. Michael Joseph. 1946.

Countryside Character. Harman, R. 2 colour plates. Blandford. 1946.

British Game. Vesey-Fitzgerald, 1 colour plate. Collins. 1946.

And Clouds Flying. Pitman, I. 2 colour plates, 51 line drawings and 8 b/w photographs of paintings. Faber. 1947.

Lemuel. Gregorson, R. 250 copies, special edition, signed by author and illustrator. 31 drawings. Owl Press. 1947.

The Frontier of A Barony. Pitt, F. Gloucester, Bellows. 1 b/w illustration. 1948.

A New Race of the Whitefronted Goose. British Ornithologist's Club, Bulletin, vol. 68 no. 6. with Dalgety, C. 7 b/w illustrations 1948.

Book of Rules. Severn Wildfowl Trust. 5 b/w illustrations. 1948.

Birds in London. Ministry of Works. Report by the Committee on Bird Sanctuaries in the Royal Parks. 1939–47. Cover illustration. 1948.

Prospectus. Severn Wildfowl Trust. Colour cover and 7 b/w illustrations. 1948.

The Jungle is Neutral. Chapman, F.S. b/w frontispiece. Chatto and Windus. 1949.

Birds in London. Ministry of Works. Report by the Committee on Bird Sanctuaries in the Royal Parks 1948. Cover illustration. 1949.

Birds in London. Ministry of Works. Report by the Committee on Bird Sanctuaries in the Royal Parks 1949. Cover illustration. 1950.

Birds in London. Ministry of Works. Report by the Committee on Bird Sanctuaries in the Royal Parks 1950. Cover illustration. 1951.

Prospectus. Wildfowl Trust. Colour cover and back. 1951.

The Mandarin Duck. Savage, C. Colour frontispiece. A&C. Black 1952.

The Fulmar. Fisher, J. Colour frontispiece. Collins. 1952.

The Popular Handbook of British Birds. Hollom, P.A.D. 9 colour plates. Witherby. 1952.

National Wildfowl Counts 1952–54. Atkinson-Willes, G. 8 b/w illustrations. Wildfowl Trust. 1954.

Waterfowl of the World. Delacour, J. 4 vols. 66 colour plates. Country Life. 1954–64.

National Wildfowl Counts 1954–55. 16 b/w illustrations. Dursley, Wildfowl Trust. 1955.

The Morlo. Knight, L.A. 2 colour plates and 30 b/w illustrations. Gryphon. 1956.

Wildfowl Trust at Slimbridge. Wildfowl Trust. 2 colour illustrations 1956.

The Grey Geese Call. Powell, B. 1 photograph. Barrie & Jenkins. 1956.

Tales of a Wildfowler. Cadman, A. 42 b/w illustrations. Collins. 1957.

National Wildfowl Counts, Fourth Report. Atkinson-Willes. G.. 14 b/w illustrations. Dursley, Wildfowl Trust. 1957.

Book of Rules. Wildfowl Trust. 4 b/w illustrations. Dursley. 1958.

The Popular Handbook of Rarer British Birds. Hollom, P.A.D. 2 colour plates. Witherby. 1960.

The New Wildfowler. Sedgwick, N., and others. 1 colour frontispiece. Barrie & Jenkins. 1961.

Down the Long Wind. Christian, G. Dust wrapper illustration in colour. Newnes. 1961.

The Story of the Wildfowl Trust. Wildfowl Trust. Colour cover illustration. Dursley. 1961.

Wildlife in Danger. Bond, Brooke. 50 colour tea-cards with 2 colour covers and 20 b/w illustrations. 1963.

Wildfowl in Great Britain. Atkinson-Wills, G. 15 colour plates and 70 b/w illustrations. H.M.S.O. 1963.

The Shell Bird Book. Fisher, J. 1 colour plate. Ebury. 1966.

An Introduction to the Collection and Work. Wildfowl Trust. 17 b/w illustrations. Dursley. 1968.

The Red Book, Wildlife in Danger. Fisher, J. & others. 9 colour drawings and 7 b/w illustrations. Collins. 1969.

The New Wildfowler in the 70s. Sedgwick, N. & others. 2 colour plates. Barrie & Jenkins. 1970.

The Wild Swans at Slimbridge. Wildfowl Trust. 1 colour cover and 2 b/w illustrations. 1970.

Wildlife Crisis. Prince Philip, H.R.H. and Fisher, J. 7 b/w illustrations. Arcadia. 1971.

Fishwatchers Guide to West Atlantic Coral Reefs. Chaplin. C. 23 colour plates. Livingston Publishing Co. Pennsylvania, U.S.A. 1972.

Guide to Centre Wildfowl Trust. Colour cover and 9 b/w illustrations. 1973.

In Search of the Eider. Driver, P. 1 b/w plate. Saturn. 1974.

Flamingos. Kear, J and Duplaix-Hall, N. 1 colour plate and 6 b/w illustrations. Berkhampsted, Poyser. 1975.

The Loch Ness Story. Witchell, N. Colour dust wrapper, 2nd edition only. Suffolk, Dalton, 1976. Revised paperback edition with colour cover 1989.

The Birdman, Memories of Birds. Douglas-Home, H. 12 b/w illustrations. Collins. 1977.

Birds of the Western Palearctic. Cramp, S. and others. Vol. 1. 8 colour plates. Oxford University Press. 1977.

The Penitent Butchers. Fitter, R.S.R. 10 b/w illustrations and dust wrapper illustrations. Collins. 1978.

Special Appeal Brochure. Wildfowl Trust. 2 colour and 2 b/w illustrations. 1979.

First Technical Meeting on Western Palearctic Migratory Bird Management. 2 b/w illustrations. Slimbridge, International Waterfowl Research Bureau. 1979.

Wildfowl and Wader Counts 1979–80. Salmon, D. ed. Nympsfield, Wildfowl Trust. 1980.

The Hawaian Goose. Kear, J and Berger, A.J. 17 b/w illustrations Calton, Poyser. 1980.

Second International Swan Symposium. Matthews, G.V.T. and Smart, M. (Proceedings.) 2 b/w illustrations. Slimbridge, International Waterfowl Research Bureau. 1981.

Saving the Animals. Stonehouse, B. Endpaper illustration.

Weidenfeld & Nicholson. 1981.

Where Wild Geese Fly. McCullagh, S. 1 colour and 14 b/w illustrations. St Albans, Hart-Davis. 1981.

Wildfowl and Wader Counts 1981–2. Salmon, D. ed. 5 b/w illustrations. Nympsfield, Wildfowl Trust. 1982.

The Wildfowl of Britain and Europe. Ogilvie, M. 7 colour plates. Oxford University Press. 1982.

Second European Woodcock and Snipe Workshop. Kalchreuter, H. ed. (Proceedings). 1 b/w illustration. Slimbridge, International Waterfowl Research Bureau. 1983.

Enjoying Ornithology. Hickling, R. 9 b/w illustrations. Calton, Poyser. 1983.

Wildfowl and Wader Counts 1982–83. Salmon, D. ed. Cover illustration. Slimbridge, Wildfowl Trust. 1983.

Bird Navigation, the Solution to a Mystery. Baker, R. Colour cover illustration. Hodder & Stoughton. 1984.

Souvenir Booklet. Wildfowl Trust. Colour cover with b/w illustrations 1985.

Wildfowl and Wader Counts 1984–85. Salmon, D. and Moser, M. ed. Cover illustration. Slimbridge, Wildfowl Trust. 1985.

Results of the I.W.R.B. International Waterfowl Census 1967–1983. 2 b/w cover illustrations. Slimbridge. International Waterfowl Research Bureau. 1986.

Barnacle Goose Project: 1986 Report. Owen, M. Cover illustration. Nympsfield, Wildfowl Trust. 1987.

Wildfowl and Wader Counts 1986–87. Salmon, D. and others. ed. Cover illustration. Nympsfield, Wildfowl Trust. 1987.

Souvenir Booklet. Wildfowl Trust. Colour cover with b/w illustrations. 1987.

Avian Genetics. Cooke, F. and Buckley, P.A. Cover illustration. Academic Press. 1988.

3. Books Containing Contributions

The New Naturalist. Fisher, J. 'The migration of wild Geese.' 3 b/w illustrations. Collins, 1948.

The Encyclopedia of British Birds. Koch, L. ed. Contributor. Waverley. 1955.

The B.B.C. Naturalist. Hawkins, D. ed. 'Painting Wild Birds.' 2 b/w illustrations. Rathbone. 1957.

The Second B.B.C. Naturalist. Hawkins, D. ed. 'Fishwatching.' 3 b/w illustrations. Adprint. 1960.

A New Dictionary of Birds. Landsborough Thomson, A. Contributor. 2 plates, 1 in colour. Nelson. 1964.

Yearbook 1968. World Wildlife Fund. 'Otters in Danger.' 1969.

The Twelfth Man. Boddey, M. ed. 'The Pond.' 3 b/w illustrations. Cassell. 1971.

World Wildlife Yearbook 1970–71. Jackson, P. ed. 'Tenth anniversary year 1971.' Morges, Switzerland, World Wildlife Fund. 1972.

1973 International Zoo Yearbook. Duplaix-Hall, N. ed. 'Reconciling the irreconcilable – wildfowl and people.' 7 b/w illustrations. Zoological Society of London. 1973.

World Wildlife Yearbook 1971–72. Jackson, P. ed. 'World Wildlife Tenth Birthday Address.' Morges, Switzerland, World Wildlife Fund. 1973.

A Dictionary of Birds. Campbell, B. and Lack, E. ed. Contributor. 1 b/w plate. Calton, Poyser. 1985.

4. A Selection of Articles from Journals and Magazines

'Wild Geese.' *Country Life*. 5 mono photographs of paintings. 24 Aug 1929.

'Wild Geese and Ducks.' *Country Life*. 6 mono photographs of paintings. 30 Nov 1929.

'Mr. Spriggs and the Crane.' *Cornhill Magazine*. Oct 1934.

'Barnacle Bill.' *Country Life Annual, 'Country Fair'*. 1 colour illustration. 1938.

'Snow Geese.' *Country Life*. 1940.

'The Magic of Wild Geese.' *Animal Pictorial*. 1 colour plate. Autumn 1945.

'Wild Geese in Winter.' *Times*. 6 Dec 1947.

'The Severn Wildfowl Trust.' *Gloucestershire Countryside*. 3 photographs. Jan/Mar 1948.

'Catching Wild Geese.' *Country Life*. 2 April 1948.

'Duck Decoys and Wild Geese.' *Illustrated London News*. 26 June 1948.

'Happy Ending to an Arctic Expedition.' *New Chronicle*. 14 Nov 1949.

'The Mysterious Sense of Direction.' *London Mystery Magazine*. 5 b/w illustrations. 1950.

'Over Manitoba Marshes.' *The Beaver*. 5 mono photographs of paintings. Sep 1951.

'To Save the Hawaian Goose.' *Times*. Illustrated with photographs. 2 June 1952.

'Wild Geese in Icelandic Fells.' *Times*. 26 Aug 1953.

'Catching Wild Geese with Rocket Nets.' *Country Life*. 29 Sep 1955.

'For Gold C Completed.' *Sailplane and Gliding Magazine*. Aug 1958.

'Straight and Level Please.' *Sailplane and Gliding Magazine*. Oct 1958.

Woman's Journal. Cover illustration, repeated inside. Feb 1959.

'Slimbridge, Winter Home of the Wild Geese.' *Meccano Magazine*. 5 photographs. July 1959.

'I Live in Gloucestershire.' *Homes and Gardens*. Illustrated. 1960.

'Nature of Fear.' *Argosy*. March 1960.

'Search for Salvadoris Duck.' *Animals Magazine*. vol. 5 no. 4.

'Skin Diving: A New World.' *Animals Magazine*. vol. 5 no. 5.

'Sightseeing in East Africa's Game Parks.' *Animals Magazine*. vol. 5 no. 6.

'Peter Scott in Kenya.' *Animals Magazine*. vol. 5 no. 7.

Birds Magazine. Colour cover illustration. Mar/April 1967.

Birds Magazine. Colour cover illustration. Spring 1978.

'The Call of the Wild Geese.' *Birds Magazine*. 4 illustrations. Autumn 1980.